LIVEculture

How Creative Leaders Grow The
Cultures They Want

LIVEculture

How Creative Leaders Grow The Cultures They Want

Nancy K. Napier with The Gang

The Gang

Jamie Cooper • Mark Hofflund • Don Kemper • Bob Lokken •
Rich Raimondi • Gary Raney • Leon Rice • John Michael
Schert

CCI
PRESS
BOISE STATE
UNIVERSITY

PUBLISHED BY CCI PRESS
Boise State University

Managing Editor: Stephanie Chism
Production Managers: Joshua Davis and Madison Motzner
Cover designer: Jackie Presnell

ISBN 10: 0-9899231-1-8
ISBN 13: 978-0-9899231-1-8

CCI Press - http://cobe.boisestate.edu/cci/cci-press/

In Memory of Bong Shin (1942-1992)
As he once said, "You can make a difference
and see your tracks from here." Thanks much
to you, Bong, we continue to try.

Table of Contents

Introduction

Culture as Competitive Advantage

[Culture] is the most underappreciated aspect of business…and the most valuable.

Walter Robb
CEO, Whole Foods,
Speech at Boise State University, September 6, 2013

On June 18, 2005—five months, eight days, two hours and five minutes after Gary Raney was elected Sheriff of Ada County, Idaho—the jail's most dangerous inmate ever escaped and remained on the run for ten days. Not a great way to start a new term as Sheriff.

Raney had been working at the Ada County Sheriff's Office for decades before the incident happened, rising through the ranks and gaining knowledge along the way. Perhaps Raney expected a fairly easy time of running an organization he knew so intimately.

No such luck.

In the post-mortem of the incident, when the escapee was safely back in a maximum security cell, Raney had several rude awakenings. On the surface level, there were breaches of security, and the call for better discipline and locks. But Raney suspected problems ran much deeper than that, all the way to the organization's culture.

Raney discovered what he calls "the cancer of complacency, more fundamental than just beefing up security." An attitude of "we are good, no need to worry" had permeated and poisoned the jail because, until the escape, the jail *had* run smoothly. There were no suicides, no escapes, and no unreasonable use of force or other major problems.

Harlan Hale's escape shattered the shiny track record. To combat the complacent attitudes and atrophied discipline left in the wake of the escape, Raney and his leadership team started an intensive process to reshape the culture within the jail. All 300+ members of the jail staff, including commissioned and noncommissioned staff, collectively revamped the organizational culture. They offered ideas to build into the mindset, with fear of complacency being one of the biggest. Raney and his team helped the jail staff build the culture—and together, to live it.

* * *

You can't change culture in months. It just takes time.

Chris Petersen
Head football coach, University of Washington
Idaho Statesman, April 26, 2015

It took about two years to get the new jail culture in place, and another several years to make it a habit throughout the full organization—on both the jail and patrol side. Raney continues to think and talk about culture. It's become an aspect that the sheriff's office is known for, both locally and nationally, which comes up in recruiting efforts, and when the office's innovation and high performance come up in discussion. The culture is an intangible asset many consider crucial for the organization to continue improving and remain anti-complacent. According to Raney, you can't just "create it and leave it there." The culture has to be nurtured like a fragile and valuable plant.

A hot topic of discussion among leaders is what it takes to kill an organizational culture they've worked hard to build. Raney experienced this firsthand in the sheriff's office when he replaced a long-term senior employee who retired. Promoting from within is one of the key values of the office, but this time Raney and his staff couldn't find anybody ready for the promotion. So, they turned the search into an opportunity to bring in new experiences and ideas, and searched externally for a director.

A national search yielded a great hire. The new director came with 25 years of experience from a similarly sized organization—also in a somewhat isolated western U.S. region. The candidate had outstanding recommendations, was excited about the new challenge, and wanted to work at a place where it would be possible later to mentor a successor. The new hire seemed perfect in every way: a person with a great resume, who said all the right things, and was the right person at the right time in the right place.

But ... (you knew it was coming).

A year and a half later, the director moved on.

Looking back, Raney admitted the culture fit was never there. The director used the right words and said he was trying hard to adapt. But after 25 years at a more traditional, unionized organization with an authoritative management style, he just wasn't able to change enough. He could never fully adjust to Raney's participative consensus approach or recognize the critical role of non-commissioned staff (i.e., those who don't carry guns) as professionals in their own right. He tended to squelch ideas for improvement and stuck to the procedures he brought with him from his former employer.

Raney explained it only took six months for the director to begin to wear down a culture built over years of intensive effort. He admitted it was alarming that a single person was able to chip away on a hard-won culture that took years to become as creative and nurturing as it was.

As Raney and other leaders say, "if you don't focus on values and culture, they can slip away." In some cases, it happens when a new person destroys it. In other cases, it happens because leaders "look away."

* * *

If you take your eye off culture and look away—even for a moment—you'll lose it.

Don Kemper
Founder and CEO,
Healthwise

When Brian Chesky, the CEO of Airbnb, asked an investor what his single greatest piece of advice for the organization was, he was a bit taken aback. Chesky expected advice about cash flow or executing strategy.But Peter Thiel, one of his major investors, replied, "Don't f*** up the culture," and then made it clear that he had invested in Airbnb largely because of the culture.

On October 21, 2013, Chesky sent a letter to the entire Airbnb team recounting Thiel's advice and discussing the importance of culture. In his letter, Chesky offered his own definition of culture as "simply a shared way of doing something with passion." He stressed that culture was living out the core values in everything people did—from how people walked in the hallways, to how they sent emails, to how they worked together on projects. He wrote that breaking the values was "f***ing up the culture," and he credited each and every employee with the power to do that. Later, Chesky posted a copy of the letter to his blog.

It went viral.

Management guru Peter Drucker said years ago, "culture eats strategy for breakfast." While strategy is something that can be spoken and presented, culture is lived, and can be done in a deliberate, or unconscious way. It can be part of what brings in and keeps the best talent. If done well, it can be a hard thing to imitate, and thus can be a competitive advantage. And it starts with the leaders.

In an interview with the *New York Times* about his leadership philosophy, Robert Reid, CEO of Intacct, a cloud-based provider of financial management and accounting software, acknowledged his own shift in thinking about culture. In his early years in management, he believed that strategy was the driving factor for company performance. From age twenty-five, he focused on creating a strategy that would make his firm succeed. As he became more proficient in execution, he realized that people and culture were the ultimate success factors. "What really mattered was culture," he says. "If you create the best culture, [strategy and execution] will follow."

During interviews and research for our book, we also discovered that leaders of high-performing organizations devote huge proportions of their scarce executive time to growing and living the organizational culture they believe will best serve their organizations. The core examples in this book, for example, come from leaders and members of high-performing, highly creative organizations. The leaders have met regularly over several years to learn from each other and get ideas on problems their organizations or the community may face. Interestingly, when we reflected on the discussion topics that emerged over time, we realized that at least 60% of the discussion time finds its way to culture—how to shape it, spread it, and grow it.

Bottom line: creative leaders see culture as a competitive advantage. They know the culture they want and they deliberately shape and spread it. Finally, they see culture as a dynamic part of their organizations and continue to (re)shape it, spread it, and live it.

Values and Culture: Where's the Overlap?

What are core values? They're stakes in the ground. They're things you believe. They're things that you hold on to and say, "This is what I'm about." They're not something that changes every day. They're something that you believe to be true.

Walter Robb
CEO, Whole Foods
Speech at Boise State University, September 12, 2013

So what exactly is culture? What are values, for that matter? Sometimes they seem like ethereal concepts flickering in the air in front of you—one moment you feel like you've finally understood them—you have definitions on the tip of your tongue—and the next moment they vanish. Definitions range from Brian Chesney's comment that culture is "simply a shared way of doing something with passion" to a more common one of "how we do things around here." Walter Robb says culture is the "place of connection and ... the place of humanity in the business." Regardless of the specific definition, most people agree that culture and values can be crucial assets for any organization. Taking liberties with a famous Rolling Stones lyric gives us an insight into the whole culture riddle: "You can't always get what you want, but you can probably get what you deserve." And that applies to organizational culture as well.

Picture a Venn diagram with two side-by-side circles. The circle on the left represents the "values" of an organization; the circle on the right represents the "culture" of the same organization. If values are the ideals that an organization desires or aspires to, culture is the manifestation or reality of the behaviors employees exhibit within that organization. In other words, regardless of what might be desired—or stated on a wall or in a manual—culture is what happens on the ground. In a sense, culture is the lump sum of all the observable ways employees exhibit (or do not) an organization's values.

In a perfect world, the two circles would overlap closely in the Venn diagram. The values would *be* the culture. The culture would *be* the values. But that's not always the case. In fact, it may rarely be the case, except in situations where the leaders are deliberate about shaping and growing the culture they want.

Almost Perfect World

Not so Perfect World

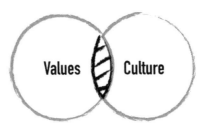

Lack of overlap may mean that an organization's values have not been cemented in employees' heads and behaviors. If leaders can make those values clear enough in terms of behaviors, and communicate behaviors in many ways throughout their organizations, then employees may begin to live the culture in ways that exhibit the values.

At its most basic, this book is the story of how creative leaders try to grow the culture they want so that it matches the values they desire. It is important to note, though, that we are talking about leaders who "grow the cultures they want," which may not always be considered "great" or "supportive" or whatever good-sounding words we use to describe cultures that some of us may wish to work in. Deliberately knowing and instilling the culture they want is what strong creative leaders do. Apple's culture under Steve Jobs was what he wanted, but may not be the culture that many high performers would want to work in. Ditto for Amazon. Jeff Bezos seems deliberate in growing a culture he wants for the firm, but again, may not be one everyone would thrive in.

Gangs, Creative Leaders and High Performing Organizations

A lot of conversations, interviews, and interactions among leaders from wildly diverse, high-performing organizations went into the making of this book. Over ninety people from over a dozen organizations gave their time and insights to help us understand how to grow cultures. The organizations themselves come from profit/non-profit and government sectors, from education to sports, law enforcement to business, the arts to health-related industries. They range in size from less than twenty employees to over 600 employees.

Many of the leaders of these organizations belong to long-term, multi-sector learning groups, which we call "gangs." These leaders of different organizations meet regularly to learn and help each other solve messy problems within their organizations or the community at large.

Many are, to put it frankly, Big Thinkers.

We want to emphasize that the ideas we talk about, the problems and solutions these leaders and organizational members come up with, can apply broadly, not just within a single organization or industry sector. Some of the organizations are larger than others. Some are in the not-for-profit world. They vary on demographics and purposes. For example, two are in education (high school and university), which means their "turnover rate" is 25% per year as students come and go. One is no longer a true start-up, since it has been in business for five years, but it continues to grow exponentially, at least 25% annually. Two of the organizations boast CEOs who have been named Innovator of the Year in their home state of Idaho. And all of these leaders are ardently committed to aggressive learning and doing things differently to get better.

They belong to an informal group called The Gang:

- *Ada County Sheriff's Office (ACSO)*—The sheriff's office has become known for innovative practices in areas such as jail management, communication, and inmate housing, drawing the attention of many other law enforcement agencies nationwide.
- *Bishop Kelly High School (BK)*—Bishop Kelly is a highly-ranked Catholic high school, which often reports 100% of its graduates going on to college. Bishop Kelly's relatively new president spent 25 years as an executive at Hewlett-Packard before joining the school.
- *Boise State University's Men's Basketball Program*—In recent years, the program has gone to the NCAA tournament and is gaining attention for some of its approaches to playing, practicing, and even naming positions.
- *Drake Cooper*—This marketing and advertising firm consistently wins regional and national advertising awards, building a powerhouse of creative output for a variety of clients. Drake Cooper recently purchased a

leader in the gamification world and will build that into future advertising and marketing campaigns.

- *Healthwise*—As a global provider of health information for top health plans, care management companies, hospitals, and consumer health portals, Healthwise leads the country in innovative approaches toward healthcare information, and incorporating tactics like Information Therapy (Ix).

- *The Idaho Shakespeare Festival*—Used as the focus of a Yale Drama School case study, the Festival has pioneered an unusual and highly successful business model, bringing financial and creative benefits to regional theaters in Idaho, Ohio, and Nevada.

- *WhiteCloud Analytics*—The analytics firm provides information for the U.S. healthcare industry to help dramatically reduce waste and increase quality of patient care. Before starting WhiteCloud, its CEO sold his business analytics firm, ProClarity, to the world's largest software company—Microsoft.

John Michael Schert, former executive director, dancer and co-founder of Trey McIntyre Project, continues as a Gang member, albeit from afar. He now teaches creative process to MBA students in his post as the first visiting artist and social entrepreneur at the University of Chicago's Booth School of Business. He is also an executive director of Treefort Music Festival in Boise, ID.

These organizations and individuals have several specific key qualities. They all share the same remote region in the Pacific Northwest, succeeding within their own fields in spite of the disadvantages of a remote location. The organizations' leaders regularly share ideas and solutions that may be old news in one sector, but new news in another. Many share values like integrity or teamwork, although they may play out differently. Last, the leaders share a passion for improving their organizations' cultures.

In addition to this group, we drew upon other organizations and people. We used many examples from Create Common Good, a social enterprise that trains individuals with barriers to employment in how to grow and prepare food and how to work in the food industry. We also use examples from a previous Gang member, former Boise State head football coach Chris Petersen, who moved (with the bulk of his organizational leaders—other coaches) to the University of Washington's football program.

The newest Boise State head football coach, Bryan Harsin, has also offered insights on changes he is making in the program that tie into culture. In his first year as a head coach, he took his team to a bowl game win and finished the season ranked sixteenth in the U.S. top football programs.

* * *

As my father has said for years, "Know who you are, what you want, where you want to go, and who you want to go with."

John Michael Schert
Visiting artist and social entrepreneur
University of Chicago Booth School of Business
Quoting his father, H. Daniel Schert

Mr. H. Daniel Schert's quote has long made good sense for his son, but it's something that can be useful as well for creative leaders growing the cultures they want. To make this work, a leader needs to know what his or her organization is in terms of purpose or mission, what it wants in terms of vision, where it wants to go in terms of strategy, and who it wants to travel with in terms of who to hire. That's the essence of the ideas in this book on shaping, spreading and growing organizational culture.

LIVEculture has three main sections, which reflect a general process of growing cultures. Part I focuses on shaping the values of an organization into the behaviors that will help instill the culture. Organizational leaders need to do this deliberately and in concrete terms. This means they need to translate conceptual, often generic, values into behaviors and actions that they expect from employees. Since culture is the way employees act within organizations, it is critical for leaders to know what behaviors they want, and to be sure they are clear to employees.

In Part II, we discuss how creative leaders spread or communicate the culture. Of course, the best organizational leaders realize this is an ongoing process. It takes time, attention, and effort to grow cultures (and less time to kill them, as we learned from the sheriff's office example). In part this is because the message needs to be conveyed multiple times and in multiple ways. Essentially, the more ways leaders can convey the expectations about the behaviors and culture they want, through different approaches, the more likely and the quicker that culture can become part of the organizational way of doing things.

Part III talks about how to grow and live the culture in a meaningful way. Again, this takes work, attention and time, especially when the culture changes, as in the jail after the escape by the dangerous inmate. The reinforcement of culture comes in the daily actions and interactions, in at least four ways: (1) how leaders encourage people to practice behaviors that reflect the organization's values; (2) who and how the organization hires; (3) how the organization reacts when something goes wrong, like having toxic employees or clients; (4) and how the organization measures whether it is making progress on increasing the overlap between values and culture.

When the behaviors become "habit," an organization's culture begins to be ingrained. This is a danger point, however. At that stage, a leader may feel it's safe to "look away," to put her focus elsewhere. Not a good idea. As the Gang leaders have learned, they need to continually focus on culture to be sure the one they want continues and is sustainable.

What Makes *LIVEculture* a Different Kind of Book?

LIVEculture seeks to help creative leaders grow the cultures they want. Note that we say they grow the "cultures they want," which may not be cultures that many people would want to work for. As we mentioned earlier, Apple under Steve Jobs or Amazon under Jeff Bezos reflect the very distinct cultures that those very creative leaders wanted within their organizations. In Apple's case, Jobs had the vision and designated specialized groups to work separately on hardware or software, rather than working together. Since Jobs' death in 2011, Tim Cook has reshaped Apple's culture to reduce infighting, to encourage collaboration and perfect execution. He is a creative leader growing a culture that *he* wants within Apple.

Likewise, Bezos has shaped a culture at Amazon that could be perceived as cutthroat in its relentless focus on the customer, and is not a culture where some people would choose to work, but it gets the job done. A fundamental assumption is that the cultures will develop an organization in ways that the leaders see as good for the organization, however they define that—perhaps growth, performance, ability to attract talent or money.

We've structured *LIVEculture* a bit differently from many books about organizations. First, we draw on lessons from very different industries and fields, to illustrate that the ideas cross all sorts of settings and organizations. Second, we've made the book easy to access and read by making chapters short and snappy and by using many examples and stories about how leaders have grown their organization's cultures. Last, because we see the power of storytelling and images becoming so important for many leaders, we use them ourselves to help convey our message.

Lessons from different fields. Many books and articles about organizational culture focus on a single sector, usually business, in the examples and challenges. But we've learned over time that creative leaders, no matter what the industry sector, face similar challenges. So, by the very nature of the core cases we draw upon, from law enforcement to education to sports to business and beyond, we want to make the point that creative leaders come from all sorts of organizations and can find ways to grow the cultures they want.

Easy to access. This book is deliberately short and, we hope, easy to read. We find that busy creative leaders and aggressive learners don't have time these days for long reads. Each chapter includes short incidents or examples to illustrate a key point in how creative leaders grow the cultures they want. The ideas are straightforward, but as our leaders make clear, they can be hard to execute and consistently follow through. They are worth taking time to talk and think about, and to help that, we've included questions at the end of key sections to keep you mulling and, we hope, to spark action.

Visuals and metaphors. One of the initial questions when we began this project was how leaders can and do convey culture in multiple ways. Gone are the days when simply saying "we value integrity" was enough. Employees need something to hold onto, something more concrete to use when they act. Also, given the research on the many ways of learning (e.g., words, visuals, experiential), we tried to find out how organizational leaders spread culture in different formats. Many use visuals, stories and metaphors.

We have followed some of our own advice and will use a metaphor of a petri dish to illustrate the process of growing cultures. So put on your scientist cap, and get ready to move into the lab, at least for a while, as we return to Biology 101.

Petri Dishes as a Way to Think About Growing Cultures

In the world of metaphors, simple petri dishes may offer insight into how leaders can grow cultures. But first, let's take a quick stroll down biology class memory lane.

Recall that a petri dish is a round, shallow, usually glass dish with a tight lid that scientists use to grow bacteria so they can learn how to treat or disable bad ones, like *e coli*, or how to cultivate good ones. The bacteria grow in colonies, and several different types can grow within a single dish. Key elements in the process include: (1) creating the environment; (2) spreading the mix; and (3) watching it grow. Let's review each of these steps and link them to organizations.

To create the environment in a petri dish, the scientist takes three steps to prepare—laying the agar, adding the medium, and inserting bacteria.

Start with the foundation. To grow bacteria colonies, the scientist starts with a gelatin-like substance called agar, which is a kind of base or foundation for the dish. In our metaphor of the petri dish, this is like the mission and values within an organization, the stable foundation or base upon which the other elements come into play.

Good biologists know they should use multiple petri dishes to assess the impact of different variables on the growth of bacteria colonies. The idea of multiple petri dishes, then, is like subcultures within an organization. Given the different variables that may come into play, units could have quite different subcultures.

Add the nutrients. The scientist then adds the medium or nutrients into the agar. This, in essence, creates the environment that nourishes (or inhibits) bacteria growth. The medium for a petri dish can range from elements like amino acids to blood to salt or other factors that will affect bacteria growth. In an organization, the equivalent would be placing a manager into a unit, department or the organization as a whole. That person then assumes responsibility for creating an environment that optimizes the growth of behaviors that will generate the desired culture. But clearly, managers can vary on several elements of leadership style, which may in turn affect the environment. Factors like the balance of positive and negative energy she brings, the way she balances perspective in terms of helping organizational members see a bigger or more focused picture, and the way she balances power (holds it or gives it away), may all affect trust and ultimately, behaviors.

Insert the behaviors. For a scientist, the next step is to insert bacteria into the petri dishes. In the organizational equivalent, the behaviors are the concrete evidence or action showing organizational values. But, of course, even with the same foundation or values, the environment may differ across units. That means behaviors that emerge could be better or worse fits.

Spread the message. In biology, a scientist will spread the agar, medium, and bacteria to mix the elements. In an organization, it's a bit different but spreading still happens. In the organization's case, leaders spread or convey the behaviors they want and expect, and that reflect the values. The spreading process in the organization involves multiple methods (e.g., talking about the culture, showing it visually, having people experience culture).

Watch it grow. Creative leaders who are deliberate about growing the cultures they want, need to watch and monitor the culture as it grows. This step is a tricky one, of course, because as the culture grows and evolves, the leaders need to find ways to encourage the culture they want. They can do this by encouraging people to practice the behaviors the culture demands, by hiring people that fit, and by being alert to how the culture is developing or changing.

Deal with toxins. In a petri dish, good and bad bacteria may grow. At some point, the scientist has a decision to make: how to deal with the bad toxins. Several approaches are common. First, he could remove, clean and reinsert them. Second, he could remove the toxic bacteria altogether. Third, he could move the good bacteria to another site and finally, he could put more good bacteria into the dish, hoping to "swamp" the toxic ones.

Likewise, behaviors inside the organization may be harmful to the culture. It is important to deal with them and some of the methods may be similar, including readjusting or training people with toxic behaviors, removing toxic behaviors or people, or adding more people with good behaviors to overpower those who are toxic.

Culture may also face contaminants of a different sort, such as pressures from outside the unit, new technologies, market demands, or competition, all of which could affect the way the culture grows.

Check the results to see what works. Last, a scientist will assess what happened in the petri dish and with the experiment. Likewise, leaders in organizations need to assess whether the culture they have—the one they hoped to shape—is what they want. If so, they can reinforce it (hiring, practicing the desired behaviors) or (re)shape or change it.

Ready to build your petri dish? Let's look at how to shape it in the next section.

Part I

SHAPE THE CULTURE

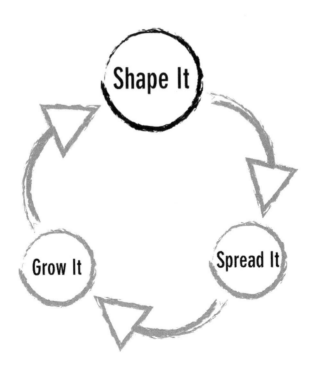

Chapter 1

Culture on Purpose

"Who do you play for?"
"I play for the United States of America!"

Miracle on Ice, 1981

The 1980 U.S. Olympic hockey team had just been beaten in a playoff game against the Norwegians, and Coach Herb Brooks was making his young players race back and forth across the hockey rink. It was late at night; the players were angry, exhausted, and sagging to the point of collapse. Hours passed. Each time they raced to the end of the rink and turned around to return, their heads sank further into their shoulders. The assistant coach blew the whistle and shouted, "Again!" to the players, forcing them down and back another time. Eventually even he wanted to stop the agonizing exercise.

"Who do you play for?" Coach Brooks asked the players.

"Boston University!"

"Cornell University!"

"Buffalo!"

Brooks shouted, "Again!"

And the players went down the rink and back again.

Finally, when Brooks asked "who do you play for?" forward Mike Eruzione said, "I play for the United States of America!"

Coach Brooks had his answer. Only then did it dawn on the other players what Brooks had been aiming for. He wanted the players to skate together—as one united team—the American team, not as individuals from their respective colleges and universities. From that point forward, the team gelled, and the result was one of the most exciting sports stories in the 20th century. The scrappy U.S. hockey team went on to an unexpected defeat of the Russians and the Finns in the 1980 Olympic Games. From the moment Eruzione said he played for the United States of America, the culture of the team solidified, and the team went on to take home the Olympic gold.

The 1981 movie *Miracle on Ice* documents the phenomenal story of Herb Brooks taking the U.S. Hockey team to the gold in the 1980 Lake Placid, New York Olympics. But the gold medal game against the Finns isn't what most people remember. The real miracle was the penultimate game against the Russians—a team considered unbeatable with six out of the last seven gold medals under its belt. The Americans had little going for them. They had less talent, less strength, less experience, and fewer resources than comparable hockey teams.

So what happened? Coach Herb Brooks' ability to shape, spread and live a culture that unified a group of arrogant, young college hockey stars into a remarkable team was a miracle. At first Brooks didn't realize the international importance of what he was doing. Eventually, he realized that the team was not only representing its country as the Olympic Games intend, but also exhibiting the values that Americans needed to rekindle after the turmoil and humiliation of the late 1960s and 1970s.

Using tough mental gymnastics, Brooks built a team that discovered winning was possible. He believed in, shaped, and then instilled the values in the team through his personal example and many training exercises. In the process, he created a culture that spurred the players to unite, and allowed the U.S. team to turn Russia's invincible game against them. Brooks and his team illustrated the power of clear values—communicated into concrete actions, and the refusal to give up. The process and its results were startling, and captivating to many.

And that's what we'll talk about throughout this book: how to deliberately shape a culture based on values, how to do that so others understand and act in ways they are expected to and how to live it so that it becomes part of the organization's way of operating.

* * *

Your organization will have a culture, whether you plan it or not.

Chris Petersen
Head football coach,
University of Washington

Just as good scientists have a plan for an experiment, so too do good leaders for their values and culture. They don't just wait for something to happen. They don't look away from the culture, especially when things are going well. Yet too many once-great organizations are shadows of what they were, in part because someone at the top "looked away" and lost the organization's culture, heart, and direction. Enron, Lehman Brothers and even Hewlett-Packard lost reputations of being stars in their fields, in part because their cultures dragged them down. A culture of self-interest, personal gain, or distance from the core of the firm can bring harm.

Think About It: What can you be most deliberate about when it comes to the values that are important for your organization? And whose job is it to "be deliberate?"

Chapter 2

Lay The Foundation

We're trying to get these kids to think about values that will carry them beyond the time when the ball stops bouncing.

Leon Rice
Head coach,
Men's Basketball, Boise State University

Chad Sarmento is a farmer's son and long-time law enforcement officer in the Ada County jail. He knows what hard work means, after waking at dawn most of his life to work on his father's farm, and uses it in his law enforcement career. He has a large square reddish face, and his eyes squint when he smiles, which is often. His voice is soft, his manner is easy but if there were any problems in the Ada County jail, I'd like him to be standing nearby. He's as solid as they come, both in physical bearing and in values.

Those values are part of what brought him to the Ada County jail and he tells his story with gusto. As we mentioned in the introduction to the book, the jail's most dangerous inmate escaped on June 18, 2005, just a few months after Gary Raney took over as sheriff. Harlan Hale was on the run for ten days before he was caught in Wyoming. During that time, Sheriff Raney gave daily updates on the local news station, and Chad Sarmento watched, transfixed. At the time, he was a leader in another county sheriff's office, on the way to a solid career and pension. He was shocked at Raney's early comments, and that the sheriff took responsibility.

Never had Sarmento seen a law enforcement official so publically admit to mistakes. He was astonished and fascinated. The more he watched and asked about Raney's organization, the more he became like a moth attracted to light. He eventually applied to join the Ada County Sheriff's Office and left his other senior leadership post to accept a lower level, lower paying base deputy job. He believed that Raney and the Ada County Sheriff's office embodied his values:

> *I believe very strongly that there are two things we swear to. One is upholding the laws, and the other is ethics in our jobs. When I put on the uniform and put on the badge, I feel good about it. Even when we get bumped around, the integrity and honesty make me proud. And the uniform I hang on my door in our bedroom—it means something to me and something to my family.*

Sarmento found those values at the sheriff's office and stays because he sees them reflected in the culture every day. They represent the foundation from which the organization builds the actions of all of its members.

* * *

> *If you have the values to fall back on, you will feel comfortable with the outcome, even if it doesn't work out the way you hoped.*

Thomas Bropleh
Former Boise State men's basketball player,
now with Finke Baskets, Paderborn, Germany

Starting with the assumption that mission is clear, good leaders think deliberately about values that support the mission—what to choose, how to frame them, and how to translate them into action. Jess Lee, who runs the fashion website Polyvore, says that one of the first things she did in founding her company was to write down the three values that were critical for the organization: delight the user, do a few things well, and make an impact.

Likewise, Jacqueline Novogratz, CEO of the Acumen Fund, also told *The New York Times's* Adam Bryant that people at her firm "wear our values on our sleeves." They seek to be very transparent and accountable, especially since the organization's members work with poor communities, where listening to their concerns is key. Novogratz says the organization positions its values in pairs to acknowledge the tension that can exist. So the values include "listening and leadership, accountability and generosity, humility and audacity." She insists that using pairs makes clear the importance of carrying out both sets of values.

Values that work build a sense of being part of something that is bigger than the current situation, bigger than a single person. When biostatistician Bonnie Lind left a 10,000-employee hospital system to join a 30-person start-up, many of her colleagues thought she was crazy. She probably did as well. But then she heard CEO Bob Lokken talk about what he hoped to build with WhiteCloud:

> *At the beginning, we went through several sessions where Bob talked about what was important to him. In some places, it's just lip service: 'Here's our mission and here are our values and now let's talk about the important stuff.' At WhiteCloud, it was: 'This is who we are and this is important to us, so you really need to get this.'*

Perhaps for Lind, part of the experience was moving to a much smaller site, where she played a critical and very visible role. What she did mattered and she knew it: "Here, there's a huge sense of personal responsibility. If I don't pull my weight, the company might not make it." As Lind says, many organizational leaders pay lip service to values and culture and then make the comment, "Now let's get onto the important stuff," which is the business of doing business. At WhiteCloud, values are the fundamental starting point. Like the agar in a petri dish, making the foundation upon which the rest of the dish is built, mission and values become the base from which culture—and the business of doing business—come about.

Other entrepreneurs think the same way, in terms of creating organizations and cultures *they* believe in. Tara Russell, founder and chief executive officer of Create Common Good, has a hard core business background. After receiving an engineering degree from Georgia Tech University, she worked for a range of firms, including Intel and Nike. She and her husband lived in Bangkok for several years before moving to Boise, Idaho, to be nearer family and raise their children.

When she started Create Common Good, she created a clear purpose (to train refugees and help them find work in the food industry), and then went about setting values and culture in a way that reflected who she was and what she wanted to build as an organization. As she says, "I wanted to build the values and culture of a place where I would want to work." That attracted others who think the same way. Chef Brent Southcombe ran top restaurants in Australia before settling in Boise to work with CCG. It was, for him, night and day: "We are a bunch of misfits, coming from corporate backgrounds. We've seen how corporations treat people and we don't like it, so we created our own culture."

Values are important for leaders and many have chosen to focus on a critical few. Rather than have seven or nine values, many leaders try to collapse or consolidate the number of values into a smaller, more easily remembered set. Chris Petersen, football coach, has used three core values—unity, integrity, accountability. Healthwise uses three—respect, teamwork, do the right thing. Drake Cooper's leaders and employees use the term "family" to encapsulate much of what they see as culture. Create Common Good focuses on "gratefulness."

When defensive coach Danny Henderson joined Boise State's Men's Basketball program, one of the aspects of leadership he felt most passionate about was building a strong culture. He had been a top performing high school coach in Texas, had built quite a following of supporters and people who wanted to learn from him, and even publishes (and continues to) a regular email sent to hundreds of people. The key topics in his emails frequently deal with the importance of and how to build a culture within a basketball program. Deliberate and continual focus on culture figure into the Boise program as well, and Henderson is a big part of it.

At Bishop Kelly High School, the leaders felt so strongly about the importance of many values that they generated eight. After a year of discussion with others inside and outside of the school about how to bring the number down, the leaders decided they could not and didn't want to. So instead of shrinking the number, they decided to choose one or two at a time and focus on those over the course of a semester or year.

The crucial point is that creative leaders deliberately select the values for the organization, take steps to be sure that organizational members know what they are, and then find ways to make those typically vague and abstract concepts into something that is concrete and meaningful.

Think About It: What are the top three values of your organization? If you can't write them down—or quote them easily—why not? How would you make them clear and explain why they matter?

Chapter 3

Add the Nutrients

Good company in a journey makes the way seem shorter.

Izaak Walton (1593-1683)
The Compleat Angler (1653)

As Walton suggests, good company on a journey makes it go faster, and presumably in a smoother manner. Likewise in growing a culture, the creative leader will find that having the people she wants helps the process go faster, and presumably more smoothly.

Those leaders of specific areas, become the equivalent of the medium in a petri dish. In a dish, the medium is the collection of nutrients that a scientist adds to the base agar. These could include blood, amino acids, salt, or any number of other factors that will affect the ability of bacteria to grow. In an organization, the medium represents the style of a given leader within a unit. While the organization may have a common foundation or base of values, different subunits may develop their own subcultures or variations of how those values are interpreted.

Part of the way those variations occur may stem from the style of the leader within a subunit. The way that a leader makes decisions, interacts with others, or builds trust can all play a role. Sometimes, the leaders or managers do not acknowledge or take responsibility for the impact they may have on shaping and growing the culture their organizational creative leaders want.

While management and leadership style can vary on many factors, we focus on three, since they can range widely and are highly dependent upon an individual leader of a unit. These three factors or nutrients that a leader brings into a unit include areas of balance managers choose to emphasize.

- *Energy balance*—The extent to which a leader brings and encourages positive energy over negative.
- *Perspective balance*—The extent to which a leader emphasizes the whole organization (big picture) over the unit's specific focus.
- *Power balance*—The extent to which a leader exhibits and builds trust, by holding or giving away power, through sharing information, decision making, and welcoming ideas from all levels.

Energy Balance

The "PE ratio" is a brainchild of WhiteCloud CEO Bob Lokken, who monitors his organization's culture very deliberately. It refers to an intuitive assessment of the level of friction that a manager will tolerate within a unit or team or organization. As he says, this PE ratio is:

> *Not the financial ratio of price-earnings … in fact, I like the contrast to that and NOT being about money. Our PE ratio would be positive energy divided by negative energy. The goal is to maximize the ratio by increasing the positive energy and eliminating negative energy.*

Lokken is an engineer's engineer with a fairly large right side of the brain as well. But sometimes the engineering side of him takes over. If he gets wound up, he describes the PE ratio as an engineer would: "The mathematics properties of the formula also have dynamics that you get a bigger effect from reducing the negative than increasing the positive by the same amount; one negative person has a MUCH larger negative impact than one person's positive impact."

Research supports Lokken's idea. Authors like Daniel Goleman, author of *Emotional Intelligence,* and researchers Marcial Losada and Barbara Fredrickson, talk about the benefits of positive emotional atmospheres and cultures. A general ratio is 3:1, meaning that environments where three times as many positive emotions exist for every negative one, helps teams and organizations perform better.

Key to this, however, is what the manager of a unit brings into the "petri dish" of that unit. Managers and leaders will vary in their energy balance, and that might influence how culture comes to play.

One other way of looking at the energy balance comes from former Boise Inc, CEO Alexander Toeldte. His terms are exothermic (give off energy) and endothermic (absorb energy). Again, though, the sense is that some people are energy producers—they are people that others gain from and want to be around, while some people drain energy from a group or person. Different managers and leaders will exhibit different levels of personal energy balance. It is a key leadership task to ensure that any team has a positive energy balance, no matter what the leader's personal style is.

The energy balance question really comes down to how much friction or negative energy a leader will allow to infiltrate the unit. How does the manager model the balance that is desirable? Will a manager identify negative energy and deal with it or let it ride? That decision will affect the behaviors of employees and in turn, the culture.

Perspective Balance

Some leaders argue that the best cultures are ones where employees care about something beyond themselves. So perspective balance refers to how a manager encourages team members to see and understand the bigger picture of the organization's purpose.

In Boise State basketball, the coaches try to instill in the players that they are involved in something bigger than themselves—the team, the program, the university and the community. That means pulling each other up and working together. As the coaches tell it, if your teammate is falling off a cliff and both of you are holding onto a rope, how long and how hard will you hold on? It's going to be painful, it will hurt you to hold on and pull him back up, so what will you do? For Ryan Watkins, former Boise State basketball player, now with Aris Leeuwarden, of the Dutch Basketball League, holding the rope became part of the way he saw the environment:

> *We have this thing called 'hold the rope.' When we work out, it's tough. And you can either give up and let your teammates down or keep going. If you are holding the rope, everyone else is on the other end. It's hard to hold the rope. But you do it because it's helping everyone else.*

Rather than create an environment where an employee may focus solely on her own performance (bonuses) that may, in fact, be a determent to the unit or the organization as a whole, to what degree does the manager encourage a broader view? How does the manager encourage, if called for, a cross-unit or cross-functional approach? How does the manager help employees understand the organization as a whole, what its goals are, what the values are, and how those play out for the unit and for the single person?

Drake Cooper combines the energy balance and perspective balance into another dimension that comes through on performance evaluations. There is a question about how an employee contributes to the organizational culture in a positive way. Again, this is an opportunity for employees to have a larger perspective about the firm, to consider that they are a part of something bigger than their own jobs, a project, a unit, and to see how they may influence the entire organization.

Power Balance

Last, an individual leader can vary on how much he holds close or gives away power, whether decision making or finding ideas that in turn can build trust (or not).

First, how transparent is the manager with communication and information about the unit and about the organization? For Roman Stanek, CEO of GoodData, having an open calendar shifts power and breeds transparency. Employees are free to see all of the meetings he schedules and, to his surprise, they are quite interested. He also invites employees to decide on a few questions that he will address in a weekly meeting. As he says, such actions build trust, which is key for the firm's culture.

Second, power balance considers how inclusive a leader is about bringing his subordinates into discussions, and truly taking their input and ideas into account, in decision making and planning. At its most basic, this refers to the control that a leader holds in terms of information, communication and time. Those can also affect decisions and empowerment down the line.

Finally, does a manager empower and offer his subordinates both responsibility and accountability to make decisions about aspects that affect the unit? We don't normally think of law enforcement agencies as ones where trust and power would be "given away." But a legendary story within the Ada County Sheriff's Office suggest that this may very true, in large part because of the environment or "nutrients" within the patrol unit.

On a Saturday night, an officer stopped two teenage boys who were speeding on a highway near their high-end suburban neighborhood. He gave each boy a ticket, told them to go home and talk to their parents. The next day, the officer (unprompted) visited each household to find out how the families were reacting, what the parents and children would do going forward regarding the infraction. In each case, he decided the response was positive and asked the boys to bring him the tickets, which he tore up. The result was a much more impactful weekend in which the officer focused on the goal of educating the young men rather than punishing them. All of this was possible because the unit leader trusted and gave power to the officer to make the decision at the point of contact, rather than insisting decisions be made from the home headquarters, or that the officer be forced to follow a "rule" than might not have applied in that setting.

 Think About It: What type of balance—in energy, perspective and power—do your leaders bring to their individual units? What's the impact?

Chapter 4

Insert the Behaviors

Suit the action to the word, the word to the action.

William Shakespeare (1564-1616)
Hamlet, Act iii, Scene 2

A critical step in shaping the culture is for leaders to translate the values, which are words, into observable behaviors or actions that leaders want. While it sounds easy, it is not. Let's look at an example. Everyone knows what "doing the right thing" means, right? Perhaps not.

For years, Nancy worked in Vietnam, helping to establish the country's first international standard business school. Part of the work involved delivering her university's MBA program to professors at a Vietnamese university so they in turn could develop and deliver a Vietnamese language masters in business to upcoming Vietnamese managers, allowing Vietnam to begin to do business with the rest of the world. But teaching what seemed obvious in the U.S. did not always seem so obvious in another country and culture.

One day, a Vietnamese participant in the program asked a hypothetical question: "What if I worked for a bank and then left to take another job. When I left my former employer, I took some money and gave it to my friend to build a house. Does that happen in America?"

Nancy's reaction, sorry to say, was pretty much a knee jerk, "Oh no. That's not doing the right thing. That would never happen in the U.S. It's called embezzling and it's illegal. You'd go to jail!"

But the participant wasn't finished with his argument.

"But I worked at the bank, I helped the bank make money, so part of it is mine, and I'm giving it to my friend to help him. That is also doing the right thing, do you not agree?"

Many other Vietnamese in the room nodded as though this was a perfectly logical rationale.

Boom. His idea of doing the right thing was so different from Nancy's. How could that be?

That was an aha moment about the need to realize that abstract values that seem clear to some people or in some settings may not be clear or interpreted the same way by others. A phrase like "doing the right thing," has quite different meanings in different contexts, and for people with different experiences. So too with organizational values, especially if they are broad and abstract. The act of translating those values into observable, concrete actions then becomes critical.

The words used for organizational values are typically big and important sounding, like *integrity, respect, teamwork, responsibility.* Even when they are widely spouted, they may not always translate into behaviors that people see, understand and can adapt to. Or, people from different backgrounds may interpret the values in different ways. So it's critical for leaders to be sure those words and the ideas behind them are clear.

* * *

As far as shaping culture, this step of translating abstract values into concrete actions is one of the most difficult and yet one of the most important. It demands discussion, time, and attention for many reasons. First, as Nancy's Vietnam aha experience showed, we cannot assume that a value means the same to different groups of people. "Doing the right thing," "being responsible," or "teamwork" could mean very different actions to different people. So leaders need to be very deliberate in thinking through and articulating what behaviors they expect to reflect values.

The process of figuring out what the behaviors should be, and in turn what that means for culture, takes time. Drake Cooper's creative director, Jennie Myers, and her team spent much of a year translating values into actions reflecting the culture:

> *We met as a team and went through a number of exercises to see how the company values translated into the team values, and how the team values translated into culture. We talk about it regularly. The process took about eight months, and I realized that bringing everyone along the whole way is important. It's not easy and it's not fast. You need to talk about it over and over again, so you sound like a broken record. And the follow-through is incredibly important.*

In the men's basketball program at Boise State University, head coach Leon Rice asked his players to "come up with the team identity," which in turn reflected values of the program. During 2012, the team members came up with the acronym TATS: "together, aggressive, tough and scrappy," as a way to remember who they were as a team and what it meant in terms of how they played. As player Anthony Drimic said:

> *Without culture, the team has no identity. And without identity, you can't play well. You need to trust each other and it shows on the court and translates into good play. Like trusting your teammates to make a good play so you don't have to do it all yourself.*

Finally, Rice uses one other way of turning values into very concrete actions. Since one program and team value is teamwork or working "together," he uses a yearly peer evaluation that the players do to cement that idea. Rice has all players evaluate each other on two key questions:

- Who do you *like* to play with?
- Who *don't* you like to play with?

Talk about a wake up call for the players. It becomes clear very quickly which ones embody the idea of being part of a team, of "huddling tighter," who tries to make that happen, and who may inhibit it.

* * *

Bishop Kelly High School leaders, staff, students and parents chose to focus on one value for a year and picked the value of "building a caring environment." That means that custodians keep the building clean, safe, and they interact with the kids when they can. Parents refrain from outbursts at sporting or other events. Teachers and students watch for any indications of bullying or students feeling isolated. Cafeteria employees talk with students in the lunch line. Every action was one that helped to build a caring environment, which meant that each group identified actions that could be explicit, clear and celebrated.

Boise State University's football program is not the biggest, fastest or best funded in the country. Not by a long shot. So the program has, over the years, focused on finding ways to bring a group together to make it a team. One way former coach Chris Petersen did that was to focus on a key value of "unity," encouraging players to become a sort of "band of brothers," rather than remain splintered into positions or class levels (seniors versus first-year students). As a veteran player said, "You'll work harder, play harder for each other if it's someone you know, rather than if it's just another person on the team."

During fall training, Petersen showed them what he meant by unity. In a meeting, he asked two players to stand. Then he asked each to tell about the other.

"What's his name? Where's he from? What's his favorite food? What's his sister's name? What's his major?"

If a player failed to answer those basic questions about a teammate, it meant the entire group paid a price—running steps, doing extra push-ups, or going through longer weight sessions. As one coach said after that happened a few times, there was a buzz in the locker room as players started asking each other questions to get to know one another. The key was to bring the whole group of just over 100 young men together so they would think of themselves as depending upon—and supporting—one another. They became a stronger group, showing more unity of purpose as a result.

Even a setting as diverse as Shakespearean theater follows the same process of translating values into action. At the Idaho Shakespeare Festival, the values of being professional, flexible, and engaged with the audience come through very clearly in the behaviors of actors, especially when something goes wrong.

For actors who have not performed in an outdoor theater, they quickly realize that they are able to *see* the audience, often for at least half of the performance, because the sun sets late in the summer. Director Mark Hofflund says the fact that actors can see audience reactions and attention (or lack of), and hear laughter makes the experience even more powerful.

And when something unexpected happens—such as an eagle sighting, a skunk crossing stage right, a flock of noisy geese overhead, or a sudden thunderstorm unfolding—both the actors and the audience exhibit professionalism and flexibility by staying *with* the performance, by having a sense of humor at uncontrollable Mother Nature, and by finding ways to celebrate the toughness of the actors and their fans.

 Think About It: What is one example of how you directly link an organizational value, like integrity or respect, to an action or behavior that reflects the culture?

Summary of Shape The Culture

[Culture is] very important, and most business people just miss it. It's something that has to be continually invested in and which can be lost very quickly if you don't keep integrity with it."

Walter Robb
CEO, Whole Foods
Boise State University, September 13, 2013

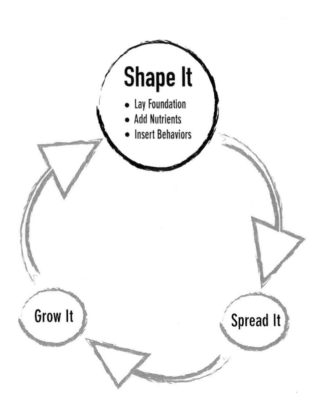

Part II

SPREAD THE CULTURE

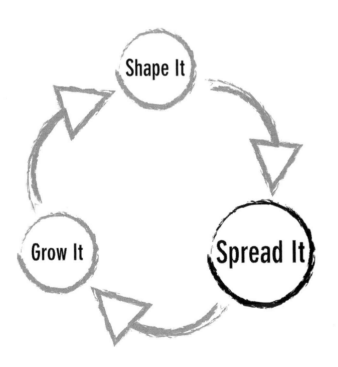

Chapter 5

Culture in Motion

Just walking down the hallway conveys something about a person and something about a culture.

John Michael Schert
Visiting artist and social entrepreneur,
University of Chicago Booth School of Business

When Nancy first asked leaders how they communicate culture in their organizations, most had a similar response: "I talk about it *all the time*. And I *model* it so people know what to do."

Excellent methods but maybe a bit too narrow for several reasons. First, people often misremember or misinterpret what they see or hear. Our brains, our memories can sometimes fail us. Recent research, reported in *The Economist*, about the accuracy of eye witnesses to crimes suggests that people reframe and change stories as they retell them. Many people, for example, "remember" seeing the first World Trade Tower being struck, and yet, the live TV cameras and videos didn't begin broadcasting until after the tower had been attacked. Our brains have reordered what we saw (second tower first) to put the event in time appropriate order (first tower first). What we think we remember, what we think we understand, is very often simply wrong. If it happens in a memorable event like September 11, 2001, what might happen when people try to remember or interpret words or modeling by leaders?

Second, since people vary by demographics and learning styles, we need communication in different forms. For example, some younger people, including university football and basketball athletes, men about eighteen to twenty-three years old, don't want to be talked "to" or "at." Making the situation even more complex, some may try to multitask (or think they are), meaning that little of what they think they hear actually makes it into their heads. Having lived for years in an environment of visual stimuli, words alone may not cut it anymore. So if leaders "talk about culture" a lot, will younger people even notice?

Third, modeling behavior is hard enough for a leader to do consistently, but understanding and grasping the meaning of that behavior can be even harder for others. The ability to interpret behaviors of others takes time and brain development. Younger people and people from different backgrounds may simply not have the experience to do such sophisticated analysis. As a result, modeling behavior may not yield the full effect that a leader seeks.

If leaders limit their communication approaches to "talking and walking" the values they want others to absorb, they may miss demographic groups of people, let alone those who learn in ways other than hearing and noticing behavior.

In discussions with football and basketball coaches and players over the years, Nancy observed how teams practice and then she watched the coaches teach techniques using a process of "hear it, see it, do it. Repeat." First, coaches talk to players about a new play or technique: "You need to keep your head cocked, feet positioned, as you move to the left." Next, the coaches show, and players watch on their own time, film clips that illustrate how good players have carried out a certain play or move. Finally, the coaches take players onto the field or out on a court, walk them through a play and then have them run it, or do and experience it.

The "hear it, see it, do it" way of communicating achieves several goals. First, it gives the player multiple chances to learn something. Most people need repetition since few of us can grasp knowledge or a skill with just one try.

In addition, the repetition is done using different means, senses, and approaches to learning. "Hear it, see it, do it" has an advantage of offering different ways to learn for people who may thrive in or embrace one approach over another. For the visual learner, the film clips help cement what he hears and does. For the kinesthetic learner, the hearing and seeing may just support what really clicks for him—experiencing a move. So in a way, the learning net is wider as more approaches emerge.

Even more so, the "see it" part of the teaching technique supports players who use visuals, even during a game. In both basketball and football, hand signals or boards are a common way to communicate during the noise and excitement of play. In football, often two players or coaches send signals to the quarterback on which play to use. One sends the "true" play, and one sends the "fake" play, to baffle the opponent. Likewise, visuals are critical in basketball, as Boise State's assistant basketball coach John Rillie:

> *Communication—verbal and nonverbal—is imperative. Especially if you are playing in an environment that is very loud, you need nonverbal communication. You'll see that on the sidelines a lot. We have signals of what we want to happen.*

So, after a period of watching and listening to coaches, Nancy asked why the coaches did not use the same range of teaching techniques to convey intangible ideas like culture. Even though they are so sophisticated in teaching football techniques, for example, coaches did not initially see the application of the same concept (multiple teaching methods) as being useful for getting across intangible ideas like values and culture. They are masters at using those formats for tangible skills but had not fully realized they could more deliberately use them for communicating less skill-based concepts.

Interestingly, even in knowledge-based organizations like software firms, visuals and alternative communication methods are emerging as being valuable and desirable. Such organizations are filled with very smart, very analytical, very "left-brained" people, and you might expect that *talking* about values and culture would be enough. Reaching the analytical part of the brain should be obvious as a way to get concepts across. Yet, even leaders in those types of organizations began to see the power of multiple methods, especially visual, in communicating intangibles.

Even more interesting, after we began to look into how leaders and employees actually *do* spread values and culture, we realized many leaders, even in sports, were using more variation in their communication than they been consciously aware of. The key going forward was to be more deliberate and systematic about communication methods for different situations.

The ultimate challenge, then, is a simply stated one, if not simply executed: Why not use multiple communications means to convey values and cultures?

 Think About It: What ways do you currently use to spread ideas of values and culture? When have those methods worked and not worked? Why?

Chapter 6

Hear It

Speech is power: speech is to persuade, to convert, to compel.

Ralph Waldo Emerson
American Essayist, 1876

Words come into play in communicating culture through reading them and hearing them when someone talks. So how do they show up in impactful ways?

Read About It

When Vicki Sullivan, management assistant for the Boise State football program, shows visitors around the football complex, she has a dramatic way of showing the impact, right from the start of the tour. You walk into the main lobby and come face to face with five glass-encased six-foot-tall mannequins, each fully outfitted in one of the team uniforms—from the famous all blue, to the infamous all black, to mixes of grey and blue and orange in between. She'll point to the trophies from conference championships and bowl games that fill the cabinets on the left-hand wall. She talks about the photo of one of the special team members carrying a hammer that fills the two-story wall at the back of the room. And then, she'll turn around, and the visitors do too. On the entry wall is an intense looking bronco head, the program's mascot, which dominates the top half of the two-story wall. The bottom half of the wall lists major donors to the building. But smack in the middle, just under the Bronco head is a phrase, all caps, with letters a foot high:

THE CULTURE IS CONTAGIOUS

And it is. From fans to donors, students to players, the culture is something that people notice and talk about. Phrases that suggest "culture" sprinkle the walls of the building—in the hallways, workout and locker rooms. The hallway leading toward the famous blue field includes a strip of that same turf with a sign above it that says, simply, "Protect the Blue." As they leave the locker room, players swipe the blue turf with their hands.

The weight room is another two story space, with two "Bad Ass" (the name of the manufacturer) ceiling fans, rows of free weight stands from Turkey, all with small decals of Boise bronco heads on the center of the weights, and waist-high refrigerators filled with juice and energy drinks. At the back of the room, in blue paint, faded to look worn and well-loved, are the words "Blue Collar," indicating an attitude that conveys work ethic, getting the job done without complaints, and having to work harder than the competition.

Indeed, during the design of the football complex, many people thought about what to put on the walls. As former coach Chris Petersen told the *Idaho Statesman,* "… it matters [what goes into the building] … I want the words to indoctrinate [these kids] into what we're all about and *our culture."* (Italics added.)

Similarly, at Healthwise, the walls are covered with lists of values or culture elements. A graphic of the Healthwise Way, which covers five key components of culture, appears in every conference room, in common areas, and on most employees' office walls. Bishop Kelly uses posters in classrooms, listing values from the "BK Way" and from the

Knight's Code, a play on the school's mascot. When it first opened, Create Common Good had the single word "GRATEFUL" written in large script on the front office wall, black lettering, inescapable on a lime green shiny surface.

Great words. Great inspiration.

Unfortunately, what seems to happen with words on the wall is that over time they become the equivalent of furniture, almost unseen and unnoticed unless they change, or unless others (usually outsiders) ask about them. The words are there, but many employees admit they no longer notice the graphics after a while, confirming the importance of using multiple forms of communication.

Talk About It

Leaders naturally use talking as the default way to communicate values and culture within their organizations. It's necessary, to be sure, but we know from advertising research that people often don't "hear" what they are told the first time, or third or even fifth time they receive a message. It takes some people at least seven times to even register an ad before they take note of and remember it. So some organizational leaders encourage employees to spend time talking about culture, which helps them build it into their ways of behaving.

Drake Cooper consistently wins advertising awards throughout the Pacific Northwest, and has been a multiyear winner of *Outside Magazine's* "best places to work" designation. In spite of the professional successes, though, many employees say the firm's values and culture were the major reasons they joined—not the golden reputation.

After a recent short meeting about values and culture at the agency, CEO Jamie Cooper sent an email asking employees what culture meant for them. Over the next week, many employees wrote in. It was clear they *wanted* to talk about culture. Brand manager Malia Cramer, listed many ways Drake Cooper's culture shows up, including ways that might seem funky to outsiders:

> *Friday 9:00 a.m. smoothies or mimosas, BrADDYs [internal awards], FB posts and groups, cyclepubs, raft trips, Outside magazine [award], Christmas parties, writable surfaces, soup potluck throwdowns, wine-days, friendly MiM competition [i.e. May in Motion: a competition of who travels the most miles by bike or alternative transportation], standing and sitting desks, bike corrals, and more ...*

Cramer also noted employees' trust and respect for each other—and their legitimate enjoyment of the people around them:

> *People here like people. We purposely didn't choose to be in a dark room alone. We are a 'please and thank you' culture and a 'smile and say hello' culture. We are friendly and kind by nature, albeit sarcastically sardonic for good measure. We're a family, especially in the sense that we can talk about our problems and how we're going to fix them, but no one else is allowed to say it or we'll beat you up.*

But it took a relative newcomer to the firm, Matt Shifley, a few days to build up the courage to share his thoughts. He says he still has "that new-guy-at-the-office smell on me." So he was fascinated by the email stream and jumped in to explain why he joined Drake Cooper. Shifley had been a stay-at-home dad for nearly five years, working from his home office in sweatpants. He was skeptical about giving up that sort of freedom when he heard about the Search Marketing Coordinator position. But during the interview process and after spending time at the firm, he "felt a good vibe." As he says, "I decided to take a leap of faith and gave it a shot." He hasn't looked back.

In the emails that flew around the company for a week, a clear sense of warmth and wit comes through. It's obvious the Drake Cooper employees are sharing experiences that make them happy, but also makes them productive. They've bonded, have their own inside jokes, and call themselves a "tribe." Several mentioned that one person, Dan Ronfeld, really is the "glue for the firm." He makes the culture come alive in fun and meaningful ways, from putting up witty signs to the way he manages the office. And when values and culture work and support the firm's purpose, it can be a powerful, albeit rather intangible, secret weapon.

* * *

Healthwise leaders use what they call a Culture Check for every six months at the organization. Employees complete a survey about how well they think the organization is doing, and a large part of it queries whether people see values being lived through the culture and actions. The survey responses are anonymous, and many employees write extensive comments. Sometimes those comments are harsh. But every executive looks at the survey and comments and must respond to the comments that fall under his or her area. They do this at a meeting that leaders call a "fireside chat," where employees hear about how the executives will address each point raised—whether and how they will change something or, if they are unable to change it, reasons why.

At software start-up WhiteCloud, employees remember early days when founder and CEO Bob Lokken spent a lot of time talking about what was important for him in the new firm. He started with the well-known pyramid from John Wooden, famed basketball coach of UCLA, which uses values that he found were critical to building a successful and long lasting program. Lokken revised the pyramid to fit the new firm and then "talked about it a lot," as he says and employees confirm. In Bonnie Lind's case, the words worked in large part because Lokken made sure people understood the values were the important part of what they were doing. As Lind says, "I think Bob [Lokken] really wants a certain kind of company, and he wants certain people who buy into the values and mission … it's not lip service here and that's clear."

Think About It: How does your organization use words to convey culture? Words in written or oral form? Do employees understand the culture just from words? What else could you use?

Chapter 7

See It

The extent to which the image used to describe a company's culture by employees matches the branding of the company, is directly correlated to the success of the leader's ability to drive and develop the culture he wants.

Rich Stuppy
Chief operating officer,
Kount, Inc

In the Boise State men's basketball locker room, on one of the walls—twenty feet long and ten feet tall—is a photo of the team, huddled together. The photo is of players' heads and their arms wrapped around each other's shoulders. They are very close together. The caption under the photo reads:

WE HUDDLE TIGHTER

When Nancy first heard this phrase, it came from a student in response to a question about "what do you think makes this program and culture different from others?" His response was, "We huddle tighter, literally." And he was right. Even a non-basketball expert could see that. When there's a stop in the play, this team comes together quickly and huddles. When head coach Leon Rice calls a time out, the players run over to where Rice sits on a small stool. The players look down at the drawings he makes on a small white board, their arms draped over each others' shoulders, their heads almost touching.

As the student said, the opponent teams sometimes seem to be daydreaming or looking around the stadium, but the Boise group has been taught to huddle tighter. He meant, of course, that the team physically huddles tighter than do other teams, but also that they try to be stronger as a team, closer as a single unit than their opponents. The belief is that as a team, they'll play better than they would as a collection of individual stars who don't coalesce.

Player Anthony Drmic sees the psychological benefit to the huddle as well:

> *It's so mental. When play stops, everyone knows to run in. Even if it doesn't matter as much for our team, it matters for the other team to see that we are staying strong. When we huddle tighter, it shows the other team and fans that we are in this together. No one is going to break us. It gives that physical image. If we can mentally wear out our opponents, it's like free points. I try to play mental games with the other team.*

This is the same young man who says that when the opposing team members make nasty comments to him during a game, he smiles. "Drives them crazy," he says.

Visuals work well generally, but especially for younger people, who have embraced visual technology like Instagram, and who appear to have shorter attention spans. Nicolas Carr, author of *The Shallows*, notes that, sure enough, our brains have plasticity that has allowed them to become less able to concentrate on longer, more complex books, articles, or thought pieces. As we build habits of rapid scanning and moving our eyes around websites, we lose the ability to focus deeply. Some claim our attention span has dropped to seconds rather than minutes. That means reading or hearing words about values and culture becomes even less appealing and, from a communication perspective, less successful at conveying the concepts and changing behaviors.

Central to this project is understanding how organizational leaders translate and then communicate desired but intangible values into a culture that people live. What we expected was that visual depictions—like the photo of tightly huddling players—would be most useful for reaching for younger people, who've been raised with lots of visual stimulation.

What we did not expect is how powerful visuals, with or without words, can be for people of all ages and backgrounds and how increasingly common they are being used.

Rachel Emma Silverman, of the *Wall Street Journal,* discovered many firms, from Facebook to Zappos to smaller software makers (e.g., Citrix Systems Inc.) use "doodling" during meetings. An artist captures the ideas being discussed by "drawing them," and adding the words. Part of the rationale is that it helps with colleagues who come from different countries, different languages, and different cultures. All can unite and (somewhat) understand concepts through visuals. Also, the drawing in meetings encourages employees to look up from their digital devices. Last, because it uses seeing, and hearing and reading, drawing helps retention.

Another example comes from IKEA, long known for innovative approaches to business. Rather than mixing visuals *and* words, IKEA uses *only* visuals in the directions that come with its furniture. It's a smart way to go. Not only do visual instructions save on the need for translation in the many languages where IKEA sells products, but again, it's a way of communicating that is universal.

As chief operating officer of Healthwise Jim Giuffre puts it, Healthwise is in the behavior change business. That means moving beyond just using words to change behaviors when it comes to health:

> *We are out to help people make better health decisions. We were in "words" for so long and now the world is about 140 characters. Last year we put a lot into video and mobile applications. That transition has been monumental and hasn't come easily. The visual success is remarkable, though. For people to look at a two-minute video and understand is incredible. We are on the cusp and interactivity has to be part of this.*

Visuals matter.

Of course, Apple has long understood the power of the visual. In his aim to blend art with technology, Steve Jobs was an early adopter of communicating visually. A 2014 *New York Times* article reported on a course within Apple to help employees understand how to design and draw very simply to generate the icons and software that Apple excels at. It uses the progression that Picasso followed as he drew bulls, from quite detailed and elaborate to very simple—just a few lines to convey the image of a bull. Picasso drew eleven versions of a bull during a single month in 1945, getting to the very clean version of ten lines with a squiggle that makes it clear the drawing is a bull, not a cow. In Apple, the point is also that developers and designers go through many versions to reach the most elegant one possible and still get the concept across.

 Think About It: Where do you use visuals in your organization? Have someone who does not work in the building walk around with you and take note of what they pick up on. You might be surprised.

The Smile Line

When Nancy visited the Shinsegae Department store in Seoul, Korea, several years ago, she noticed a brass plate on the floor, just outside an employee lounge. Every few minutes, a store employee left the lounge, in a spic and span uniform, walked to the brass plate on the ground a few feet from the lounge door and stopped just before it. Then the employee bowed slightly, straightened his or her shoulders, put on a "game face" (or better yet, a "store face") and entered the store proper.

What did the brass plate say?

"Smile line," written in English, with a smiley face at the edge. This very graphic reminder seemed to help employees stop, readjust their mindsets and their uniforms before reentering the world of work. It's almost like actors stepping onto a stage. Nancy talked about the smile line to several leaders, and some adapted the idea for their organizations. Two that use it on a regular basis are Create Common Good and the Boise State basketball program.

When employees, visitors, and donors visit the small Create Common Good offices and kitchen, they walk into an open office, with concrete flooring, and brightly painted lime green and yellow walls. About ten feet into the office, on the floor, is a strip of white with the word "Why?" painted in black on it. Like the "smile line," the "why line" helps people remember why they work, volunteer or sponsor CCG. As Chef Michelle Kwak says:

> *It is a reminder for us or anyone who comes in. It is to remember why we are here. On the days when we are frustrated, we can then remind ourselves why are we here.*

In the Boise State men's basketball locker room, a similar line appears, just as the players leave the privacy of the locker room and exit for the stadium. This line on the floor says "Passion!" As the coaches say, if you don't play with passion, there's no way you can win. They try to instill that love of the game from their early relationships with the students, but the passion line helps to remind players to give it all they can every time they head out to play a game.

The Sheriff's Five

To help him, and to help his officers remember what values they should hold, Ada County Sheriff Gary Raney keeps five artifacts on his desk. Whenever he swears in new officers, he talks about each of the symbols of the office.

- *A sheriff's five pointed metal badge*—A symbol of the trust that citizens hold for the sheriff's office, which reminds the men and women who wear the badge that they must earn and cherish that trust every day. While some sheriff's offices around the U.S. use cloth badges that attach to a shirt with Velcro, Raney insists that his officers wear a metal badge. They pin the badge to their shirts before they go on duty every day. It's hefty, it's long lasting, and it's symbolic of the longstanding trust that has built up—and that the office wants to continue.

- *A feather quill*—A symbol of the law and reminder that no one, including and especially law enforcement officers, is above it.

- *A small telescope*—A symbol that reminds officers that they are under scrutiny, that their behavior will be monitored and watched, no matter where they are, on or off-duty. As a result, they need to be above reproach and uphold the values of the organization, even when they are not on duty.

- *A compass*—A symbol of finding and holding onto one's true north. Every officer needs to be honest and show integrity. If something happens that moves an officer away from that position, the compass reminds people to "get back to your own true north."

- *A hasp from a broken lock*—This comes from the escape we discussed at the front of the book, when a dangerous inmate was able to break out of jail. To do so, he broke the hasp that sits on Raney's desk, a hasp that no one thought was breakable. That the inmate was able to take advantage of several breaches of security and then break through an "impenetrable lock" reminds people to avoid the "cancer of complacency" that became so clear after the escape.

 Think About It: If you had to come up with one image—or five—that illustrates your organization's culture, what would that be? What would it say to potential recruits? Would your image be the same as your employees' visual images?

Build a Legacy, Build a Culture

Healthwise celebrated its 30th anniversary by commissioning a sculpture called "Relentless Innovation" that sits at the building's entrance. A solid, unmoving pole stands thirty feet high, with a wrought iron windmill at the top, which moves with the wind. The pole represents the solid values, strong foundation and history of the organization. The moving windmill represents the necessity for the organization to adapt to the changing environment and move in different directions as needed.

An example from the Boise State football locker room is another that instills a sense of history and legacy. The lockers are about eight feet high, with compartments for shoes, clothes and helmets. At the top are two metal name plates. The current player's name and jersey number appear on the left side of a nameplate that is about eighteen inches long. Just to the right of it, on a matching plate about six inches long is the name of a former player, his hometown, and the years he played. As current players graduate and move on, a new player's name will appear, next to his "ancestor" player who also contributed to making the program better. Having those two names on a locker sends a message to the current player that he is part of a legacy, that he is lucky enough to be in a great facility and great program very much because of those who came before him.

At WhiteCloud, one value is growing the firm together, as a team, person by person. To illustrate that visually, each new employee receives a red brick when he or she joins the firm. The brick has the employee's name and date of employment. The bricks sit on employee desks—or wherever they choose (perhaps under a desk?)—most of the year. But at least one day a year, employees stack the bricks against a wall in the office and take a photo. The year to year photos show the growing number of bricks and people, and also signify the importance of building a firm, brick by brick, person by person.

A final example of trying to convey culture and build legacy comes from another photo in the Boise State men's basketball locker room. The twenty by ten foot photo shows the Boise men playing against a much higher rated team, the University of Nevada-Las Vegas. Boise State lost the game, in overtime. But the players felt their performance showed they deserved to be "in the game" and the photo reminds them of that. As player Jake Ness commented:

> *Everyone thought we would get blown out. It's motivating to know that if we work a little harder to do one more thing, we can win. After that game, we started playing better. The photo is a reminder.*

Their coaches talked about the performance against all odds, the players see it in the photo; they felt it during and even after the game. And it's a way they can teach each other and newer students of the power of their team culture: tough, aggressive, together and scrappy.

Think About It: What visual could you use—or do you use—that gives a sense of growth or change within the organization? What shows legacy over time?

Step on it, Week by Week

The men's basketball locker room at Boise State University is a large round room, about twenty feet in diameter: lockers around the edges, broken up by the door into the shower area, and a white board on the opposite side with an inspiration quote written before each game. In the center of the room is a rug with the bronco mascot head and border about eighteen inches wide that fronts the lockers. One day while Nancy was visiting, she watched a young student scooch around the edge of the carpet, brushing against the lockers.

What was that about?

Every week in a basketball game, coaches monitor which players "take a charge" for the team. This refers to a player who is willing to stand firm, allow an opposing player to run into him so that one of his own colleagues can shoot a basket.

Pride of honor, in a way.

For the week following a game, any player who has "taken a charge" is allowed to step onto the bronco head in the locker room. Those who have not—including those who didn't have the chance to play—must tiptoe around the edge of the carpet, staying close to the lockers but not on the bronco head. It's a reminder of who took action for the good of the team, and, of course, the people who "step on the bronco" change every week based upon player performance.

Interestingly, the notion of "interacting" with something visual has grounding in science. Nobel Prize winner Eric Kandel, a professor of brain science at Columbia University, said in an essay for *The New York Times* that this idea first appeared in 1900 when Alois Riegl of the Vienna School of Art History said art was "incomplete" without a human reacting to it. As he said, for art to succeed, it needs the viewer to exhibit both "perceptual and emotional involvement." In a sense, the viewer works "with" the artist by transforming the image into what he or she sees in the world. The art comes alive as the viewer comes alive viewing it. Sort of like a Bronco mascot head.

Think About It: Do you have any "interactive" visuals, ones that change but also ones that people can make change based on their actions?

Chapter 8

Do It

Act as if what you do makes a difference. It does.

William James (1842-1910)
Psychologist and author

Do it if You Mean it

Boise State head basketball coach Leon Rice tries to do things differently to improve, but also because he needs to find nontraditional ways to compete against programs that have more resources, taller players, and bigger schedules. A few years ago, he had one tall player—but several who were good at various tasks. As associate head coach Jeff Linder said, "We knew our best lineup was with four guards, but no guard wants to be called a (power forward)."

So instead of thinking like other teams (and using the traditional names for player positions), Rice tried to model his own culture of being innovative and finding ways to match a player's skills with what he does on the court. Part of that was conjuring up new position names:

- *Trigger*—A player who understands and knows every position, can shoot from outside, and is a sort of "glue" for the others.
- *Gunner*—A player who gets to the basket and can then attack and shoot.

- *Pusher*—Usually the first to get down the court as fast as possible.
- *Pitcher*—A strong shooter who a pusher often throws the ball to first.
- *Crash*—The "man in the middle," and one who crashes onto the boards.

The coach tries to model "doing things differently," just as he asks the same from players.

* * *

Other high performing, highly creative leaders follow similar paths of knowing the values they hold true and using them as a base upon which to build the organization's culture. A regional theater that has expanded into new markets is another good example. Mark Hofflund, managing director, Idaho Shakespeare Festival, and Charles Fee, producing artistic director, work with three regional theaters (Idaho Shakespeare Festival, Great Lakes Shakespeare Festival, and Lake Tahoe Festival). Each man started his career in acting, and then each realized he would find a better niche by shifting to management and directing.

Fee, for example, started his career in the theater more than thirty years ago. He admits now that very early on, he realized he would never be as good an actor as some of his peers. So, he shifted to directing (and eventually to running the business side of theater as well), in part so that he could create jobs for his friends. He has done that well. But his unique and extremely successful business model stems from some strong values that run counter to the normal practices in the theater world.

Fee leads three theaters that produce and transfer plays from one to another across the country over the course of a year. The Idaho and Ohio theaters have complementary seasons (not overlapping), so plays may start in one location, run for eight or twelve weeks and then shift to another location and have a similar long run. The benefits are many. As he says, it "showcases the work" nationally, it allows the directors and actors to improve the play over the course of a longer run, and very importantly, it allows him to hire artists (directors, actors, designers) and craftspeople (costumers, set builders, painters and the like) for longer timeframes, meaning that they have nine to twelve months of work and benefits. Very rare in his industry.

When he tells the story of why the business model is so important for him and the three companies, he brings up the key point about employment and benefits as one of the top reasons for pursuing what is not an easy approach. It reflects the values of the organization, and results in a culture where he can support people he respects and likes, and who do outstanding artistic work.

*   *   *

It's often the small things that leaders do to reflect values, especially if they are done consistently. At Create Common Good, being grateful is a core, and perhaps the most important, value. Visually, the word cannot be missed: on the lime green shiny painted front office wall, in large black letters is, in huge letters, the word "GRATEFUL." Scattered around the word are the names of donors and supporters.

But Create Common Good seeks other ways to show gratefulness. Employees sign off emails with "Grateful," the CEO hands out gift cards to show appreciation for jobs especially well done, and employees conscientiously show gratefulness in how they interact with each other, with simple gestures, like asking for a few minutes, rather than interrupting a co-worker. As Angie Tuft says, "that means we value each others' time, and show it every day."

* * *

The president of Bishop Kelly High School, Rich Raimondi, may lack long-term educational experience but he makes up for it with his years of executive experience at Hewlett-Packard. He worked at HP during the heydays when it rose to become one of America's great firms, then went through major economic difficulties, management changes and decline. But since he lived and loved the original "HP Way," made popular by the founders, he understood the implications such a culture had on the success of the organization. He had worked with leaders who modeled clear and strong values. He built them into his own leadership style and was ready to model such values into a new setting.

As a result, when Raimondi joined the high school, he naturally, almost intuitively, brought many of those values and ways of behaving to his new job. Partly, he exhibited the importance of respect and curiosity by not assuming he knew much about education, so he asked questions (still does) constantly. Showing up at school events, being positive even during crises, doing the right thing for the organization and its members are ways that Raimondi models the behaviors he expects from and in others. That's who he is and it shows what can be done, as director of alumni relations and marketing, Katie Kerby, noted:

> *He calls people by name. He says, "You did such a good job with this." He lifts up the maintenance guys and the gals in the cafeteria for being able to respond quickly and cheerfully to things. He'll say to all of us, "Your hard work is really paying off, everybody notices, it looks great." He thanks our parents for being patient and understanding, and thanks the IT guys. By Rich modeling that behavior for all of us, we have all gotten better at doing the same thing for our peers.*

John Michael Schert has urged mayors from Chicago to Boise to include more artists on boards, commissions, and in discussions about what the cities could become. He argues that they have perspectives that most business and government people do not, that they may bring more insight into design, and they are a growing part of most community cultural life.

His suggestions can sometimes be refreshing. For example, when cities consider adding sanitary landfills or industrial sites, why not add a "master of smell" to the design and construction team. Our sense of smell is one of the most primal, most powerful, and yet how often do we take it into account in city planning? Similarly, when it comes to transportation, could dancers help in the discussion on how people move, not just how to move people?

When Others Do It

In athletics, even students notice when the culture is different. Thomas Bropleh, former basketball player for Boise State University, now with Finke Baskets, Paderborn, Germany, remembered his first visit to the university:

> *The players treated me how they would like to be treated. They said positive things about the new coaches and they were all seniors. As seniors, that's a big deal because with new coaches that changes a lot of things. But the players liked the new coach (Rice) and his assistants, and it just felt right [for me].*

One of the ways Healthwise encourages the value of respect, teamwork, and doing the right thing is a regular Healthy Snack Day, according to learning and development vice president Carol Casler, who calls it a tradition: "It happens when we celebrate or have a big announcement that is positive. Sometimes it is just to get together. It's the idea that you can take a break to celebrate."

For employees of marketing firm Drake Cooper, the talk about being a "sustainability-focused firm" rang hollow when the firm paid for employee parking. So the company shut that down and got serious about May in Motion, a city-wide effort to encourage alternative means of transportation beyond individuals driving their own cars. Karma Jones, creative service manager, says:

> *When we moved to the new building, there was an emphasis on being 'greener.' One of the things that was high on our priority list was creating a culture that encouraged all of us to be part of the solution. To do that, we started 'Green Rewards,' a year-round program rewarding people who commute to work by foot, bike, carpool or taking public transportation. They get a cash reward every month they participate. Along with that, we participate as a company in the city's May-in-Motion program that comes with extra incentives. At Drake Cooper, that means fun, games and inter-office competition.*

And it works.

Think About It: What behaviors do you model to convey the culture you want?

Chapter 9

Teach It

"Those who know, do. Those that understand, teach."

Aristotle

If you've ever taught something to another person, you know that's the time you really learn something. Think about when you had to explain a geometry concept, or why your child should care about grammar, or what gravity is, or how to make a milk shake.

Answering any of those questions by teaching another person drives home what you mean and how you get the ideas across. It's the same with conveying culture.

Teach it and learn it. Teach it so others can learn it.

We found at least two ways this happens: leaders teaching others and peer teaching peers.

Leaders Teaching Others

Bishop Kelly High School President Rich Raimondi teaches in a very explicit and visible way. In his role as president, he regularly meets with student council leaders at the high school in an early morning weekly leadership course that a teacher offers. Raimondi joins the class periodically to talk about leadership but also about how to instill the Bishop Kelly values throughout the student body. A powerful message is, of course, that the president (not the principal, but the *president* of the entire school) considers leadership and the values of the school to be so important that he wants to teach them himself to the elected school student leaders.

Like many organizations that are heavy with Baby Boomer age leaders, Healthwise faces a situation where four to five of its senior leaders will retire within five years. Its leadership and board are highly aware of this situation and are serious about succession planning. It urged them to begin the Executive Healthwise Way program. The organization chose 16 managers, most of whom are two levels below the highest ranks, and has begun to train them as leaders. They often use case studies of real decisions that leadership has or will be making, and then ask the managers to choose and justify a solution. The younger leaders gain appreciation for what senior level jobs entail (e.g., "Wow, these decisions are harder than I thought, and you don't always get it right"). In addition, the segments on culture focused on how big a role it plays in decision making.

To make it even more meaningful, senior leaders had to agree that they would accept the decisions of the younger leaders. While this sounded like a good idea at the time, some leaders balked later. After the first strategic decision came in, several people argued against accepting it. At that point, Jim Giuffre, chief operating officer and the senior manager in charge of the development program, noted that unless leadership was willing to accept the younger managers' decisions, the development would be moot. The decision held.

Likewise, in the Ada County Sheriff's Office, some of the senior officers naturally take on that mentor/teacher role. Chad Sarmento comments that senior officers use a form of mentoring that is informal but effective. When he is in the field and sees a younger, less experienced officer handling a situation that may not go well, he waits.

Only after the situation has resolved does he pull the younger officer aside: "Let's talk about what happened.

Why did you decide to do what you did? What might you do next time?" Rather than telling, he uses questions to encourage the younger officer to review what happened and come up with an alternative himself. Also, the act of pulling the younger officer aside and talking privately maintains respect for the officer and the office. As Barry Clark says, "People learn by example, especially in this job. If they see the guys with experience doing wrong things, they think that's OK, so you just have to hold yourself to a high standard because people are watching."

Peers Teaching Others

Boise State assistant basketball coach John Rillie comments that, "It's always more empowering when it's a player teaching another player. That's why we want our former players back hanging out with our guys."

Ryan Watkins, former Boise State basketball player, now with Aris Leeuwarden, of the Dutch Basketball League, led by example. And that meant holding himself accountable for fully completing practice exercises, like running the entire length of the court, reaching down and "touching the line" before turning back to run the other direction. As he puts it:

> *The way we teach is through our actions. If we don't touch the line, they [the younger players] won't touch the line. And we [older players] have to get on them if they don't, from [learning things like] showing up on time to taking care of what's going on in class.*

Kirk White, Boise State's assistant wrestling coach, has the intensity that champions in any sport need, but it's especially evident in wrestlers. He is deliberate in his movements and wastes no energy, almost to the point where it is painful to watch him because he seems to have used his legs and knees in ways that humans should not. He was a national champion in college in his weight level, competed internationally for years, and was part of U.S. teams that went to the top first or second slots in multiple venues. He's also a thoughtful teacher who has learned how to help students teach each other.

White uses a method he calls 1-3-9 to spread information and techniques from coach to players in an efficient way. He teaches three players and they, in turn, each teach three other team members (by this time, nine have been taught). It's similar to what software firm WhiteCloud Analytics CEO Bob Lokken calls the "fractal method" of spreading knowledge. He and his senior leadership team needs to understand and exhibit a behavior to the point where it becomes a habit. They then must instill the habit or behavior into their own teams (of two or five or eight people), spreading the knowledge and behavior throughout the organization.

Similarly, Bryan Harsin, head football coach at Boise State, is fully aware of the need for players to be leaders of and for other players. Interestingly, in the lead up to Harsin's first season, the local newspaper profiled several players who were mentioned as great players but who also were stepping up to be leaders for the team. As Harsin says, he needed key players to buy into the new system, culture, and what the new coaches were trying to achieve. If he could get that core group to see the big picture and become advocates, then he expanded his reach.

 Think About It: How do peers teach peers about culture in your organization? How does onboarding happen, where new employees learn about culture?

Chapter 10

Feel It

Sometimes, when I'm trying to learn something, I create a song to help me remember.

Jake Ness
Boise State basketball player

As we've mentioned, Boise State wrestling coach Kirk White was a 1999 national champion as a university student. He has the body of a wrestler: medium height, stocky, scarred knees, and a determined look in his eyes. And when he talks, his enthusiasm for wrestling spills out. When asked about how he knows if student wrestlers understand and can do a technique correctly, White says, "I know it when I feel it. Then I help them feel it too."

In White's case, he can literally and physically *feel it* if a wrestler understands a move. He gets down on the mat with a student, where he can feel the muscles, how the wrestler acts and reacts, and can tell if the player is in the correct position for a particular move. Then he reverses it and asks the student to feel his body to get an understanding of what he's talking about.

While most business environments might not condone "feel it" in a physical sense to show values, other ways of feeling it certainly come through. In fact, the notion of feeling made sense to several leaders who use other ways to help people feel values and culture—through storytelling, physical space, metaphors and body movement.

Tell Me a Story, Touch My Heart

Robert Fabricant, vice president of creative, for Frog Design New York, sees storytelling as the "net sum of curiosity, empathy, and engagement." Good leaders know that intuitively and use stories to bring up deep emotion and understanding. From Socrates to Aesop, from William Clinton to Steve Jobs, leaders have drawn upon stories to make their points, to inspire, to set a vision that people want to follow.

Lisa Cron, author of *Wired for Story,* says that in a given moment, we may have millions of pieces of information coming at us through all of our senses. Our "conscious mind" can process about forty (or even many fewer), while our unconscious mind is busy absorbing and sifting, even though we're not aware of it. According to Cron, stories help the brain make sense of and create meaning from the incoming information. As she says, neuroscientists now can say we are indeed "wired" to make connections, put information into some order so it is understandable for us, and it allows us to imagine or experience in our minds what we may not (have to) go through in reality.

In essence, stories put us into a situation that can change how we think or act, even if we are not in the actual situation—or are never likely to be. You don't have to be stranded like Ernest Shackleton and his crew were during the 1914-17 attempt to cross Antarctica to go through a simulated experience of fear, thinking through how to lead, solve problems and (try to) come out alive. You don't need personally to go through the agony of public failure or cancer, when you can listen to Steve Jobs talk about being ousted from his firm and then dealing with life threatening (and eventually fatal) cancer.

The experience, if told—or shown—well, can generate similar emotions to what one does go through in real life. Bob Gregory, former defensive coach at Boise State and now at the University of Washington, uses the stories in film clips to communicate a point to his players. One year, to emphasize the importance of integrity and of keeping a bigger goal in mind, Gregory used a scene from the World War II movie "Saving Private Ryan," in which Tom Hanks plays a lieutenant leading a group of men whose goal is to find Private Ryan. As Gregory explained:

> *In the movie, things are chaotic. The soldiers capture a German and half the guys in Ryan's group want to kill him. But they have to move on because they're trying to save Private Ryan. [As they argue], the guys are all betting on what Tom Hank's character does in America since he's not saying anything [about himself]. [Then] Hanks tells them, 'I'm a school teacher, sixth grade. My wife's name is Annie." He opens up. In the midst of the war and chaos, he opens up and everyone stares. He says, "what we're doing here [arguing about killing the prisoner or not] is not going to help us find this young man [the main goal]. If I can get Private Ryan home, that helps me get home." The bigger goal and integrity [is what I want the players to understand]. And they get it [when they hear the story].*

Increasingly, as organizational leaders use stories, they also realize how challenging it is to train and have good storytellers. Some are seeking different types of employees as a result, as Michael Malone suggested in the *Wall Street Journal,* when he wrote that competitiveness in the business world has shifted "from engineering, which everybody can do, to storytelling, for which many fewer people have real talent."

Healthwise CEO Don Kemper says that "we're learning how to the improve storytelling capability of everybody, but particularly the leaders of the organization." Stories include five parts, according to Kemper—a problem, people, a place, progress and pictures, and they must be visual and emotional to be truly effective. "We tell stories about clients that were really upset and how we did the right thing to solve their problem—even when the fault was on their side. Helping clients find success, though often costly at the time, always pays off in the long run."

Bob Lokken, CEO of WhiteCloud, uses the story of Antarctic explorers in 1911 trying to reach the South Pole to make a point about "sticking with the program" in his firm. He compares the Norwegian (led by Roald Amundsen) and the British (led by Robert Falcon Scott) teams as they raced to the pole.

The Norwegian team had a discipline of going forward 15 nautical miles every day to preserve the strength of the men and dogs. The British, in contrast, went long stretches some days when the weather was better, and didn't move at all other days when wind or storms were bad. In the end, persistence and discipline won and the Norwegians reached the South Pole on December 11, several weeks before Scott's group, but kept it secret until they returned safely. The British reached the pole but unfortunately died on the way back, in part because they used a less disciplined approach.

An employee who heard Lokken tell the story initially thought it seemed "corny," but admitted that it worked because it "stuck" (she remembered it), and clearly made the point about staying with the company's vision, and the importance of daily persistence.

Some stories happen organically. Boise State's former football training coach, Tim Socha, now at the University of Washington, says that every summer as camp began, one of the newer players would raise the question about "who makes it." An impromptu "RIP Board" developed, where the veteran players listed previous students who were no longer in the program. They may have left because they were homesick, didn't get to play as much as they wanted, found the work to be too hard, or they fell behind academically. Writing those names on a board was a powerful teaching tool for veteran players to instill "what it takes" into the newer ones. What's also important, according to Socha, is that the *students* "tell the stories" on this one, not the coaches, which increases the impact.

Stories work in part because they do tap senses and emotions, rather than just logic. Some researchers call the heart an "emotional conductor" and mention that its electromagnetic field has 5000 times the strength as the brain. In fact, some argue that simply being around a person who is giving energy, especially positive, can make a difference in our own sense of energy. So if that's possible with stories, could it be another way to convey values and culture?

The Space Where I Want to Be

"Have you ever been to jail?"

Ask that question in a crowd of adults and the response is telling. Some people look guilty, thinking about the teenage misbehavior that landed them in booking or even a night in the jail. Others just laugh out loud. Still others look like they think the questioner has lost her mind.

The question is, of course, "have you ever been TO jail," not IN jail. Regardless, it's an invitation that few people want to pass up once they realize they may go as visitors, not inmates. Most people think jails and prisons are like the ones they've seen in *Law and Order: Special Victims Unit*, places that few would want to spend time in. Not so in Ada County. You still don't want to spend the night, but if you have to, it's quite a different experience than what we see on TV shows.

First, there are no bars on the cells. Mesh wire and glass, but no bars. Next, the floors shine and the hallways are uncluttered. The colors are soft greens; there is minimal sound and when an inmate in a single cell does call out, a deputy shows up right away to find out what's wrong. When inmates pass deputies, sergeants or the sheriff in the hallway, all of them greet each other with respect, and usually by name:

> *"Hi there, Mr. Jones, how's it going?"*
> *"Good, Deputy. How about you?"*

Likewise with the sheriff and his deputies and sergeants when they exchange small tidbits about how things are going, what's new, or whether there is anything in particular to be aware of. The entire experience surprises even jaded jail visitors. The facilities are well maintained, which reflects respect for the staff and inmates, and is one of a set of key pillars important in the jail.

The jail leaders think about more than just layout, as well. Sergeant Chad Sarmento recalls when he was working in a room with his sixteen colleagues and subordinates, and even the table(s) made a statement:

> *There were two small circle tables, to fit all sixteen people. I looked at that and then saw an eight foot long folding rectangle table in the corner. One afternoon, I took the circle tables away, and put the folding table in there. I reminded them that if we sit at the one table, we were one team.*

From then on, the team sat at one table.

Physical layout has long been a visual way that organizations seek to communicate culture. Google and Microsoft are often cited as being innovative in their use of lighting and casual furniture, bright colors, and tucked away spaces for people to sit and work, or meet and talk. Austin, Texas based company HomeAway, takes its business of vacation rentals and brings some of the feeling into the office space. Its leaders try to instill a sense of "vacation at work" so that the 500 plus employees in Austin want to come to work each day. The lobby has brown wicker deck furniture, magnets and postcards from around the world and snow globes to give a sense of fun.

Another very different firm in Texas that has made a deliberate effort to mesh layout and culture is Dynegy. As *Wall Street Journal* reporter Joann Lublin describes it, when CEO Bob Flexon joined the Houston based firm, it was going through bankruptcy. Flexon immediately took the firm out of high end, expensive office space (and eliminated the $15,000 desk in the CEO's office) to an open office where each employee, including the CEO, has a sixty-four square foot cubicle. Flexon wanted to convey openness and agility. By having everyone together, in the open space, it also helped build a sense of spirit to save and build the company again.

The architecture of Healthwise's headquarters building reflects openness and transparency. The office and conference room walls are glass. Well-behaved dogs are allowed on the campus, so the office nameplates show the employee and the dog names. As Molly Mettler, senior vice president of mission explains:

> *Healthwise has bikes in the lobby, which means "Your health is important." We have an in-house gym, a nursing mothers' room, a nap room and a hammock. We don't [have to] say respect, teamwork, and wellness—that's who we are.*

Facebook has taken the notion of layout one step further. An organization that wants its employees to get used to the idea of constant change and unpredictability, it has built that into the way the meeting spots are arranged. Throughout a main floor are clusters of furniture groupings—1960s style couches, tables and chairs that make great places for meetings, and employees use them. But to keep the level of ambiguity and non-predictability high, the furniture clusters move periodically. So just imagine saying to a colleague, "Yeah, let's have a meeting at the green couch area like we did last week," and then you show up and the furniture is gone. While the idea is clever, you have to wonder if some productivity loss comes from people searching for new places to sit and hold meetings!

Create Common Good uses color, space and dress to reflect values. The offices are open, the desks are uncluttered (on purpose), and the colors are bright—lime green, school bus yellow, with cement flooring. The kitchen sits next to a large meeting area, with a nearly twelve foot square table that is used for meetings and for lunch (all employees and visitors in the building eat together). The walls in the dining/meeting room are painted in shiny bright green and orange that can be written on, like white boards.

Are We A Pack of Gladiators or Kids in a Park?

Brittany Asher, business banking relationship manager for a large U.S. financial institution, sees her employer as the embodiment of the magician in the Disney film, *Fantasia*. As she says, all banks are essentially the same, in terms of what services they offer. So how does one distinguish itself from another? How does the number five bank seem different from the number four or the number ten? Partly through the visual image it presents and the culture it builds. In this case, she explained, "We're like the magician because 'we make dreams come true.' We help families afford houses and send their kids to college. We help ourselves by building careers. We make our own dreams come true, and we also help our customers' dreams come true."

Over the years, Nancy has asked groups of leaders to describe their culture—as they exist or as they would like to see them—using metaphors. Dale Pike, leader of a university IT support unit said, "We want to be an old tennis shoe. Rather than being the flashy new version or model of the latest technology, we want to be the shoe that you know, that you're comfortable with, that will get you where you want to go without blisters. Our support group should make a client feel good and safe, and that we'll go the distance with you, by your side."

Others think of culture in a multilayered way. One leader in a high technology firm founded by a family from Iran, said the firm's culture is like a Persian rug. It looks very patterned and colorful from a distance. But when you get closer or look on the back side, he said, you'll see the intricacies—the different threads and colors and how there may even be some mistakes that no one would notice except for company members. But when you stand a bit away, it looks like a beautiful integrated piece of work.

Another senior leader of large, high performing health care organization said, as a relative newcomer to the organization, he felt that he had stepped into a city park on a sunny day. Everyone in the organization was having a great time doing good work in their own units, but they were not coordinated.

One manager was experiencing an acquisition in which it was very unclear on who the winners and losers would be, who would retain a job and who would lose one. His metaphor was of a gladiator event because it felt to him that during the organization's transition, everyone was fighting one another for space, for power, for survival.

Finally, a group of graduate students describing their organizational cultures used very dynamic images, with action within them. For example, one saw her culture as a "camping trip." She said, "The group knows its destination (clear vision), knows what roles each person plays (some set up camp at night, some do the cooking, some do clean up), and recognizes that the adventure includes both fun and work." A second described the culture a little less positively, as a sandbox with kids playing with toys and tools. But when a new kid shows up, there is not much of a welcome, and the kids who have been in the box a while destroy the newcomer's sand structures, making it hard to "fit in."

In some of these latest examples, it also feels as though the cultures just emerge, rather than being a deliberate action. Culture just appears somewhat undesigned or unplanned. And that may be a good measure of how well the leaders are shaping and spreading culture: do employees throughout the organization think of it in similar ways? As a "dream maker?" As a city park?

Interestingly, when leaders do ask employees to come up with a metaphor, very often they are quite different, raising a question of what do the leaders want in culture and how are they conveying it? Or do people in different parts of the organization see its culture in strikingly different ways, and does that matter?

Beyond being an exercise for leaders to capture their own view of their organizations' cultures, it may also help leaders understand how employees see the culture. One employee said he perceived "two visuals of culture" in his organization. If the overall metaphor was of a circus, the leaders would see it from a distance, with happy people, lots of color and movement. The employee, however, said his view would be "closer up," a zoom-in perspective, showing some of the underbelly, problems, and sadness in the circus, even including fear on the faces of some people, as if they were on a roller coaster.

 Think About It: What metaphor would you use for your organization? Why? What metaphor would your employees use?

Your Body, Your Culture

Three final examples suggest that culture can be conveyed in nonverbal, often unconscious, ways. Former dancer and current social entrepreneur and creativity consultant John Michael Schert sometimes works with organizational members on ways to enhance their sense of self and creativity. One exercise involves asking people to walk through the group and have others notice.

Walking through a group when you know others are watching is hard for most people. At a session with staff members of a large institution, one woman walked briskly through the group. Schert then told her to think about what was bothering her, to ignore it and to walk through the group again. What did the others notice? She walked much more slowly. But more than that, the others said, "She seems so busy and unapproachable when she walks fast. When she's slower, I feel like I can stop her and ask a question or chat."

What was going on?

The woman worked on the first floor of the building, but said that the "more important people," who were her bosses and colleagues, worked on the fourth. When she went to the upper floor, she felt she was not respected and thus was unworthy to be on the fourth floor. As a result, she walked fast to get her work done and leave. In doing so, others read her behavior as being too busy to talk, when in fact she felt a culture that was not open and respectful.

Another example is from a very creative leader of a highly successful organization that seeks, in many different ways, to encourage innovation. Yet, at one meeting a senior manager unknowingly did just the opposite. An employee was at a conference table with several leaders and offered up an idea for discussion. The senior leader leaned back in his chair, crossed his arms, and lifted his eye brow.

People who know him well know that this is a gesture of sitting back to consider, to think, to ponder. But the employee did not know the leader and interpreted the body language in the opposite way. The leader was pulling away, closing down, and showing skepticism. All without saying a word. The employee's reaction was, "I'll never put at idea on the table again in front of him." Simple movement and gestures, done without thinking on the part of the leader but resulted in closing down any hope of future innovation from that employee. The leader, without knowing it, was conveying the exact opposite of the culture he wanted to grow.

A final example comes from basketball, which is a very physical sport to be sure, but combined with action and words, the coaches can convey the culture even more effectively. Boise State men's basketball associate coach Jeff Linder is a strong presence, and not always in a way that seems friendly. In fact, he may jump on players who appear to be complaining, who seem to be not giving their all, who may nearly talk back under their breath. As Ryan Lundgren, director of player development, explains it, Linder's action give the message especially the newest, youngest players that they are not the hottest players in the group, as they may have been in high school. It's a way to break them into the Boise State way of operating.

So in practice, Linder yells, gets into the face of a young player, and then steps back and almost ignores him. He'll cross his arms and turn away. At that point, one of the older players may come in and show the younger one how to make a move, how to position himself better to guard, or give him a quick touch to boost his energy. It looks like an exquisite dance, or good cop-bad cop routine. By showing he'll take no guff, that he has expectations of these young people that perhaps they had no inkling they could deliver, Linder is setting the culture as well. It's a message of get tough, be scrappy, be aggressive, but play together and don't try to show off. Just what the students' identity of TATS (tough, aggressive, together, scrappy) is all about.

 Think About It: Are there situations when you unintentionally hurt culture because of your actions or those of other leaders? Find someone you trust who can watch you for unintentional actions that do not convey the culture you want.

Summary of Spread The Culture

You can't sell it outside if you can't sell it inside.

Stan Slap
Under the Hood, 2015

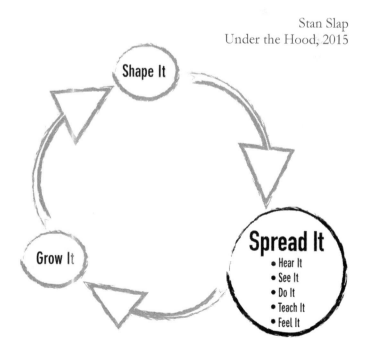

Part III

GROW THE CULTURE

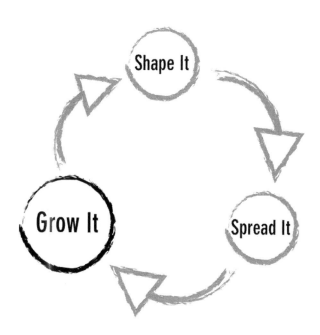

Chapter 11

Culture in Action

[The question is] do you want to go home at night? Or do you want to be dead?

Tally Cantrell
Jail deputy,
Ada County Sheriff's Office

Tally Cantrell has been a jail officer for many years at the Ada County Jail. The value of respect for all is one that she tries to practice every day, in small ways and large. She transports inmates from the jail to court or to doctor appointments. It's an assignment that can be dangerous but also is rough on the inmates emotionally. She tries to show respect, though. Her behaviors show the inmates—and the public—that the Sheriff's Office employees are trying to live the culture they profess—respect for all:

> *[We] respect the inmates, [we] don't treat them as if they are lower than other people. [For example,] when you take them to the doctor's, in the waiting area, they are already embarrassed [because they are] in chains. They don't want to go. So before we go, we explain the rules. When we go in, we sit down, and tell them what's going on. You don't talk to them like: "Sit down, go this way!" You have to show [the inmates and] the public that you care and have a heart.*

But Cantrell is not being altruistic. She lives the values because it's the right thing to do, but also because it could save her life:

When I first [came to the jail], we had a lieutenant who taught us ethics. I will never forget that he said the way you treat inmates may come back to you one day. If there is a riot in the jail, do you want to be the one where the inmate says, 'Hey, you leave that officer alone, she was respectful.' Or do you want to be the officer they are going to beat because you treated them without respect? [The question is] do you want to go home at night? Or do you want to be dead?

Instilling a culture so that it sticks is crucial, even if top leaders are gone. And to do this, we return to the idea of being deliberate. Culture does not happen by accident, and to become habit and part of an organization's way of operating requires that leaders, as well as employees within the organization follow the expectations and behaviors that make the culture live.

*   *   *

A culture is only as good as today.

Molly Mettler
Senior vice president for mission and culture,
Healthwise

Boise State head football coach Bryan Harsin arrived to great fanfare but got right to work in spring 2014. One of his areas of emphasis for the program was to build a culture he wanted and to find ways to live it every day. As he says, "you can't stop [working on it] once you've figured out what values and culture you want." His philosophy is that even after (you think) you've conveyed the values and the culture, you have to keep "spreading" them so that the players and others "own it" and live it day to day. And then, you "spread it" again.

He's right. We've learned that translating values into behaviors and then communicating them are critical to building a culture. But leaders who truly own their organization's culture live it every day. They see culture as continually growing part of their organizations that needs to be nurtured to thrive. So how does the culture become part of what people do every day?

From watching high performing, creative organizations whose leaders foster cultures they want, at least five ways are common:

- *Hire for Fit and Vet for Values*—Find people who fit the culture.

- *Don't Fall in Love*—Take your time to find the right people since the mistakes can be costly.

- *Practice with Purpose*—Practice the behaviors you want and do it deliberately and consistently.

- *Watch for Toxins*—Recognize when things aren't working and find a way to deal with it.

- *Is the Culture Working?*—Measure how the organization's culture is doing over time and decide if it needs to be (re)shaped.

Think About It: You've shaped the culture. Now, what's the biggest challenge in your organization to make sure you don't lose what you've done?

Chapter 12

Hire for Fit and Vet for Values

If you don't fit the culture that's already here, either you will be miserable or everyone else will be miserable.

Dylan Amundson
Brand and business development manager,
Drake Cooper

Amy Errett, chief executive officer and co-founder of Madison Reed, is definite about how she hires and it has everything to do with fit. People need content skills, to be sure, as she told *New York Times* reporter Adam Bryant, but what she's really after when she interviews is vetting candidates culturally, asking whether they have the same values that she and her company have. Errett wants to find the "genius" in each employee, but to start, she needs to be sure they will fit into the firm. As she told Bryant, "I just want to see that there's a soul in there, that there's some way they can make this place different, and can we weave that fabric together?"

Once again, creative leaders try to be deliberate in searching out the good fit. A misfit can sap energy, lower productivity, increase "whine-time" for people nearby, and generally cost time and money. In a business that is "all about relationships," finding the right employee—and for that matter, the right clients—is critical.

Marketing firm Drake Cooper knows it wants employee and client relationships for the long term because its leaders think they can pay off in more energy, faster and greater productivity, less complaining and more profit. So Drake Cooper hires carefully and intends for new hires to stay with them. And it pays off. While the average client stays 10 years with a firm, most stay 12 or more with Drake Cooper. Employees often jump firms in the industry but at Drake Cooper, some people have stayed for 20 years.

Leaders of firms that strive to hire for fit do seem to look deliberately for specific characteristics in candidates. Kon Leong, co-founder, president and CEO of ZL Technologies, told Adam Bryant of *The New York Times* that curiosity is one of the main characteristics he seeks. As he says, "We're trying to find the right fit. In a fast-changing environment, you need to learn on your own. And to learn on your own, you need curiosity."

Leong's idea is common for many leaders of organizations that try to do things differently to get better. When individuals notice ideas or items that they find curious, and then talk about why that is, it shows an ability to be an aggressive learner. The "something" could be political, science or art. That doesn't matter. What does matter is how a person thinks about the information. The CEO of Orbitz Worldwide, Barney Harford, looks for passion, energy and curiosity, which are more important than specific experience. As he says, "You want someone who can learn fast and who will be able to adapt as the organization adapts."

Many organizational leaders and members use informal approaches to learning about candidates and assessing fit. Software developers at health information analytics firm WhiteCloud are a tight group. They work in an open office, have periodic "Nerf ball fights," and spend time together on and off the job.

And they are very serious about finding developers who will fit into the (sub)culture they've evolved as well as in the culture of the organization as a whole. So as a final step in the interview process, developers take a candidate to lunch. They ask an applicant what type of food he (yes, usually a he) would like and then during lunch, they ask about motivations, why the person is applying to the firm, and what his free time activities are. The group will also crack a few jokes to see how the applicant reacts and to decide if they all will "like each other."

This ephemeral quality of "liking each other" has practical payoffs. Craig Boobar of WhiteCloud calls it "building the community" or "lubrication" and feels that face-to-face relationships support better performance:

> *The reason the community is important—and why people like to play and do fun things together—is that it brings down the barriers to communication and eliminates or reduces conflicts. With remote employees, you have very limited interactions with people. If you have one bad interaction, you flip, then anytime you work together, there's going to be friction. You can't help but have disagreements. How you deal with that is 'lubrication,' or building friendships and relationships in your community.*

Sports coaches have their own approaches for looking for people who will fit. Chris Petersen, head football coach at the University of Washington focuses on finding "OKGs" or "our kinda guys." That means focusing on qualities other than football skills and knowledge, more on the type of character that a young man has.

Likewise, Boise State's basketball program, under head coach Leon Rice, also wants recruits who will "fit" and he involves current players in that assessment. Anthony Drmic describes how current players get a feel for a recruit, in terms of what sort of a person he is, beyond his technical skills. The players take a recruit to an "open gym," where the coaches are not present:

*In the open gym, we get to see if the recruit meshes [with us].
Usually you can tell within ten minutes if he will fit in. You
look at how hard he plays and how much he cares. And
because it's an open gym [no coaches present], some players
don't care, but recruits should [want to] impress us.*

Think About It: How do you get at the
"real" character of a recruit to know if the
person will fit the culture?

Chapter 13

Don't Fall In Love

We wouldn't continue to recruit a kid who we felt would not eventually "get it," because his great talent could turn out to be destructive rather than constructive. Character is a significant part of our recruiting. I want [a kid] who will listen to his coach, has shown respect to his parents and other authorities and is willing to learn.

Mike Krzyzewski
Duke University head basketball coach,
Interview in *Journal of Management Education,* 2011

Of course, as we've seen, even the best of organizations may not always follow their own rules. The book's opening story about the sheriff's office unfortunate hire is, alas, an example of the dangers of finding what looks like a dream candidate for a job and sometimes letting that override potential questions about whether the individual would be a good culture fit.

Football coach Chris Petersen calls this mistake "falling in love with talent." When he was at Boise State, he recognized that the program could not recruit the biggest, fastest, or highest rated players. Too many other programs had more resources for attracting those players. When he and his coaches did find a player they thought was especially skilled and who they could really use to boost the program, he cautioned himself and others to be wary of "falling in love," rather than being steely-eyed about whether the student would fit the culture. When he didn't, the match often went sour. But there are ways to avoid that. One of the most common is staging the hiring process.

The road to becoming a member of a top college athletic program is long for most students. Coaches may begin to watch high school talent when players are in their sophomore or junior years of high school. Former Boise State coach Bob Gregory estimated the rough amount of time that he and his fellow coaches would spend recruiting a football player for Boise. Starting with a database of 1,000 kids, at different stages and ages, they typically tried to recruit 17-18 kids per year. That means a lot of review and sorting as they try to come down to a smaller group they scrutinize more seriously.

The initial review includes watching film, talking with coaches, and visiting schools. Then, the average amount of time he might spend on the most serious candidates was, conservatively, another 40 hours per student. This more thorough evaluation involves watching more film, talking with the recruit, coaches and others on the phone, and then visiting the school again. The coaches talk with the recruit's coaches, teachers, family, even the security or custodial people in a school, all in an attempt to find players who would "fit" the culture.

Fit is part of the Boise State basketball program's criteria as well. They watch and know players for years before trying to bring the best ones on board. Player Jake Ness understood that:

> *[The coaches] try to bring in guys with good character, hard working. Not a lot of guys are troubled. [The coaches] try to get everything they possibly can out of you. They want to get your best because they know you have more to give and they want to see you reach your goals.*

As CEO of a nonprofit social entrepreneurship venture, Create Common Good's Tara Russell is especially careful of hiring, partly because she cannot afford to carry people who aren't fully committed to the organization. Her staged hiring process, which she calls "date before you get married," involves moving people from volunteer to part-time employee to full-time employee.

Jen Hurt, head farmer at Create Common Good is a classic example of how the organization's hiring process can work. Health problems made Hurt realize she needed to reassess her life, including what she was able and wanted to do. Gardening was a passion and after she found her way to Idaho and to Create Common Good, she offered to volunteer. Later, she became a part-time employee and, finally, the lead experiential educator and head farmer for the garden.

Healthwise also takes its time in hiring, including a multiple day-long interview process, time spent with the CEO, senior leaders, and the vice president of mission and culture. The candidate often analyzes a case study and presents recommendations to senior leaders. Many people who apply find that it takes two or three tries to land a job at Healthwise. The process, in other words, is time and money intensive on both sides.

Even with such a thorough process, it may still take time for the new hire to understand and "fit" into the culture. In one case, Healthwise invited a senior executive from a publically held firm to join its board and later he joined Healthwise as a senior leader. As CEO Don Kemper puts it, it took a couple more years for the new executive to adjust to the Healthwise culture. In a corporate setting, he knew well how to get things done, but had to learn a different approach and culture at Healthwise. Kemper also acknowledges that the culture can be perceived as a possible barrier to hiring, but it's so important to the organization that they are willing to wait for the right candidate to fit in:

We have probably lost good candidates because of culture. We had a [senior executive] candidate that we were seriously looking at [for a year] and I think we scared her away because of culture, which is a shame. She had a really good alternative and I think she was more comfortable with that. My sense, though, is she would have converted easily over time. But when you come from another environment where you do things a different way, it's uncomfortable at first and one just doesn't know if she can do it.

The staging of hiring over time gives both sides plenty of time to see whether the work skills are there, and more importantly, whether the culture fit exists. And it allows both sides to avoid "falling in love," since they move past infatuation and get to the real work of building a relationship that will last.

Think About It: When have you "fallen in love" with a candidate and it didn't work out well? Why not? How can you avoid that?

Chapter 14

Practice with Purpose

The main thing is the main thing. Stay focused on it.

Dan Hawkins
Former Boise State head football coach,
Current ESPN commentator

In the 2015 Super Bowl game, with 50 seconds and less than six inches to the goal, the defending Seattle Seahawks made a call that would cost the game. Former coach Dan Hawkins said that the Seahawks forgot "the main thing," which was getting the ball to the guy who could make the score.

Hawkins uses that phrase, coined by Stephen Covey, when it comes to organizations as well. When leaders get distracted or take their eye off the vision, mission and culture, they're not focusing on the "main thing." And when they lose that, they no longer focus and practice it. Such focus and practice are critical on the football field or in an organization.

* * *

Natalie Shores, director of administration at WhiteCloud Analytics, knows how hard practicing can be. For two years, she and leaders at the firm have tried to identify and master key skills and behaviors as a way to build the firm's culture and turn habit into actions. For instance, the leadership team identified listening as a key skill, including something very straightforward like simply not interrupting another person. The challenge is that creating such a habit, easy as it may seem to understand, still takes effort, time, and practice. As Shores says, working on one or a few techniques a month means that building mastery in key skills and making them part of the "rhythm" of the organization can be laborious:

> *Consciously, we practice [some aspect or behavior] twenty times a month [once a day, five days a week, for four weeks]. Subconsciously, it gets into our workflow. But I would say that even our twenty times a month may not be enough time for some behaviors.*

Of course, some behaviors and actions are easier to grasp than others. You could practice listening, instead of interrupting, one hundred times a month (think five times a day, five days a week, twenty days a month). But other areas, less tangible, might take more time and effort, such as dissecting a problem using critical thinking steps. It could take months to learn it, so Shores stresses that the leaders use deliberate practice. As she explains it, "Each skill is fairly discrete [but] they build on each other, and the more I work on skills mastery and critical thinking, the more I see people demonstrating those behaviors through the learning teams and through the debrief process." Finally, if a group of people all work on practicing the same skill, they can call each other out when one of them fails.

Bishop Kelly High School, as we've mentioned, generated eight core values for the school. For a year, Rich Raimondi listened to many smart leaders tell him that eight values were too many, that three or four made more sense and were easier for people to remember and practice. So Raimondi and his leadership team tried to reduce the number of values and consolidate them. In the end, they could not. They decided that the values the school community had identified were all important. So rather than eliminate or consolidate values, they chose to focus deliberately for one year just on one value and the behaviors that supported it.

They chose "creating a safe and caring environment" as the first value to focus on. The school had faced bullying, parents who acted inappropriately at sports events, and kids who felt excluded. To help build a safe and caring environment, then, everyone associated with the school, from students and teachers, to parents and board members, to staff and administrators figured out what types of behaviors could create a caring environment. Students could help each other, could intervene in a bullying situation, or tell a teacher about it and get help. Staff or teachers or students could call out parents who might be acting inappropriately at events. Staff members might talk privately to students who needed a bit of extra attention. Cafeteria workers or custodians could ask students how they were doing in the course of their daily work.

And it worked.

Because the school as a whole had agreed to practice the behaviors relating to building a caring environment, the effort was deliberate, intentional and supported throughout. And since it was the whole school community, rather than one or a few people trying to make a change, the chance for the behaviors to become more routine and supported by everyone, they stuck. Next step? A new value and set of behaviors to focus on, while maintaining the first.

The benefit of repeated, consistent behavior that reinforces values and culture is that others within the organization are more likely to pick up the behaviors as well. The Ada County Sheriff's Office wants the community to be safer, for drivers to be better educated, and for ticket writing not to be a revenue generator. Patrick Orr, community information officer, was surprised shortly after joining the sheriff's office to realize how deeply those feelings went:

> *[The deputies] are problem solvers. They deal with kids, drug additions, and they are trying to make sure the kids are OK. I believe our deputies are really making the community better, rather than giving tickets. People believe that and they act that way, and that's how the culture evolves. You walk it and talk it, and then everybody starts to follow the same path.*

Be Consistent

Former Boise State (also now University of Washington) defensive backs football coach Jimmy Lake spent time in several different programs over the years, including in the National Football League. From one experience, he too learned the importance of consistency in building or changing a culture:

> *The head coach, who I had a lot of respect for, was very detailed, had great team meetings, knew what he was talking about, had passion, and talked a lot [about culture and values.] But then I'd walk into the locker room and see the general manager talking to players and he was not relaying the same type of information that the head coach was trying to get across. And then the other assistant general managers and some assistant coaches weren't giving the same message. Later, the head coach realized he didn't hire the right staff around him to carry out his vision and change the culture.*

Lake's story raises the question of who has responsibility for growing and living the culture. To be sure, the leaders must exhibit and live the behaviors they think are important.

Another example comes from a senior leader who followed his own organization's culture, and took responsibility for doing what it demanded, even when most people had no idea he had violated it. The CEO was leading a discussion at a breakfast powwow of high-level leaders in the local community, where the meetings are confidential, wide-ranging, and eye-opening for attendees. Nancy had brought a student to take notes (for distribution to the leaders and for research use) and to gain an inside look at the thought processes and interactions of the high performing, highly creative leaders.

At the close of the meeting, the CEO went around the table, asking each person for final comments. He asked all of the leaders but skipped over the graduate student. In previous meetings, the students were included in the discussion, where appropriate, and the other CEOs had asked if they had any final ideas for the discussion. But this CEO did not ask.

After the meeting, Nancy, the student and the CEO had a separate meeting on another topic. Before that meeting began, though, the CEO called himself out and apologized to the student.

"One of our organization's key values is 'respect for all.' I didn't honor that just now when I skipped over you. I didn't show respect. I skipped you because I forgot your name, but that's no excuse. I'm sorry." He owned the values and corrected the mistake.

Most CEOs might not make the effort to apologize. Some might not even notice that they'd skipped the student. But for that CEO and for that organization, his actions fully reflected the organization and its values. He owns the values, communicated them with his apology and tried to show that he seeks to live the culture that he and others have created.

John Rillie, Boise State assistant men's basketball coach, admits that players get into all sort of trouble, from skipping class, to showing up late for practice, to leaving their phones on during team meetings. To maintain the culture and expectations, the coaches take responsibility, at least at first. When something goes wrong, the coaches typically look to themselves:

> *The first step is [to ask,] 'How could I have helped the situation?' You are never going to improve the culture if you don't evaluate how you could help. Did we communicate? Did we give good advice? How can we help the student communicate better with the professor? Did basketball hinder his academics?*

Interestingly, though, within the same organization, the students themselves realize they must also assume responsibility. Boise State basketball player Anthony Drimic, who lives in Australia during the off season, makes that point:

> *It's on us. The coaches have some responsibility over us, but I feel like it's on us. Even through the summer, we need to keep the Boise State name [reputation]. When you commit to coming here, you need to respect it [the values] and hold it. This team has respect for the team to stay on the right track.*

 Think About It: Who has responsibility for growing culture in your organization? Do you instill that throughout the organization or do you hold it close to the leadership team? Why?

Chapter 15

Watch for Toxins

Everyone thinks they understand what the culture means until you make a wrong decision.

Donte Deayon
Boise State football player

The true stickiness of culture comes through most when something goes wrong within an organization: clients go rogue, an employee steps out of line, or subcultures clash with the organization's culture as a whole. In a science experiment, good and bad bacteria colonies may inhabit the same dish, and the ways of dealing with toxic bacteria can be fairly straightforward: remove, clean and reinsert; remove altogether; add more "good bacteria" to the mix; or move good bacteria to another dish.

Toxins may emerge in organizational cultures as well. Finding cracks in a culture or in behaviors is crucial but can be hard to see and hard to manage. So what do some of the creative leaders do?

Obviously, to enhance and cement a culture, organization members need to be consistent in their practice of behaviors and skills that reinforce it. This matters especially when something goes wrong. Sports coaches talk about doing so on and off the field. University of Washington offensive line coach Chris Strausser mirrors many of those ideas when something goes wrong and students step out of line, both on and off the field. The first thing he asks himself is whether he communicated the idea or request in a way that the players understood, bought into and could carry out. He knows that "You get what you emphasize so [use] a combination of repetition, communication and then find an even better way to communicate."

* * *

But, in the end, it comes back to the mission and values.

Drake Cooper is an organization that sees clients as partners, working together on a concept, ideas for a campaign, assessing and building an outcome together. Because the culture of working together both within and outside of the organization is so important, it can become a point of stress when the partnership falters, or never gets off the ground.

During the 2008-2010 financial crisis, Drake Cooper faced a serious decline in business, forcing leaders to make some tough choices. The biggest was what business to take on. They could accept work that would keep the firm afloat but that would not fit cleanly the type of work they normally do. Another option was to take work from organizations, like not-for-profits, that could not pay Drake Cooper's normal rate but that still respected the integrity of both Drake Cooper and the client firm. In the end, Drake Cooper's leaders decided to stay with clients that better fit them but charged somewhat less during the tightest times.

Another time, the decision came down to culture match with a client, as CEO Jamie Cooper tells it:

> *When the economy tanked, we had to set clear boundaries to uphold our values. Do we value our company's culture more than we value the revenue? It's hard enough when things are good, but those were tough times. When a client's culture starts eating our culture (in a bad way), then we need to be*

> *honest about what costs we are willing to endure for the*
> *financial benefit it provides the business. What do you put*
> *first? People or profit? The truth is both are important, but*
> *if we ultimately optimized around common business*
> *principals like "growth" and "profit," we may make some*
> *bad decisions for our culture. In my experience, this is always*
> *where culture meets its fate. Not all growth is good. Not all*
> *profit is worth the cost to obtain it.*

Drake Cooper treats people, employees and clients alike, as peers. So for Cooper, working with people who did not match those values meant either his firm would have to adapt to the client or his firm would need to "fire" the client. In his view, the best time to see how strong and serious leaders are about culture is when "something goes wrong."

If you cross the line and adapt or change in ways that do not respect the culture, the employees will know it and you'll lose the culture. Whole Foods CEO Walter Robb would concur. He too claims that the tough times are when "walking in your values" really shows (or does not). This is when "you walk away from sales to stand up for your values … that you are who you say you are."

Former Boise Inc. CEO Alexander Toeldte calls this decision point a "tight-loose balance." If a manager is "loose" on upholding the culture and values, there is no turning back. In his mind, holding "tight" to the culture is "real work" for leaders, demanding that they remain consistent to the values and culture, even when the decisions are difficult.

* * *

One winter season, the Bishop Kelly High School junior varsity basketball team had a run like never before. The team was consistently beating opponents and the students set a goal for themselves: to reach 100 points in a game.

They met the goal one afternoon, walloping their opponents, 100-29.

When school president Rich Raimondi heard about the game, he was surprised and disappointed. How could the coach and the kids have done something that was so outside of the respect and honor values that the school's community held? He used the event as a teaching moment with the coach and discussed that, even though the students may have wanted to reach such a goal and played well, it contradicted the value of respect for others. The coach recognized the mistake, wrote apologies and talked to the students about how the other team and parents must have felt, helped them understand that such actions were not "who we are." One more opportunity to cement the values and culture.

* * *

The story of the sheriff's office employee at the start of the book is a good lesson for any organization. The hints of trouble were there, but it was hard to connect the dots.

Six months into his job, the director talked with an outsider about his new position. In the twenty minute conversation at a social event, he spoke only about "how we did it in my last job." Even when prodded, he said nothing about what he was learning about his new employer and colleagues, what he thought was going well, or what he wanted to improve.

Over the course of the evening, the outsider noticed that he seemed to ask no questions of others, showed little curiosity in getting to know them, and appeared to speak *to* people, not *with* them. Within months, people who worked for him were beginning to see cracks in the culture, but it took a full eighteen months before it became clear that, even though he said he had tried, the director was unable to adjust to the new organization. Given that the position was so hard to fill and so important for the organization, it was difficult for both the director and the leadership team to admit that the person-culture fit had not worked.

The lesson during the process was that leaders, and others in an organization, need to monitor and watch for signs of culture crack, which may be in a person or even within a group.

* * *

WhiteCloud's Craig Boobar sees potential dangers of a subculture that becomes too different from the organization's culture at large. In software, the rough-and-tumble world of developers can build a tight group, almost a clique, that may become separate across the broader organization. So leaders must watch how subcultures mesh with (versus conflict with or overpower) the organization's overall values and culture.

Midcourse Corrections

When things aren't going well in a game, a lot of factors [help bring us back]. The leaders on the team, tight huddles and our coaches reminding us that we are good enough to be [in this game]. They really help. They give us our step back.

Igor Hadziomerovic
Boise State basketball player

Few organizations hire the right people all the time and have employees who always perform at high levels. So what do creative leaders do when something goes wrong, someone makes a mistake, or doesn't follow the expected values and thus harms the culture?

Organizations seem to follow several paths, partly based upon the mission, the values and culture. The Sheriff's office is quite straightforward. Major Ron Freeman of the sheriff's office says the leadership team asks first whether the behavior from an employee stems from "the head or the heart?" By that he means, does the employee simply make a mistake based on lack of training or just not knowing: that's classified as a "head" issue. The head problem requires training, retraining, or mentorship.

Or, does the employee know the difference between right and wrong and still chooses to make the wrong decision, such as lying to a supervisor or showing behavior that contradicts our values of integrity, service, dedication and attitude. You can't train such things as integrity (heart). There is no amount of training that can remedy a heart issue. If an employee has a heart issue, the sheriff's office is deliberate about letting a person go and moving forward.

Some organizations give an employee multiple chances to work things out. Not-for-profits like Create Common Good or Healthwise try hard to help employees change behavior. According to senior leaders, Create Common Good might give someone three to four chances to change and improve. Healthwise will try to find another position for an employee within the organization. In these cases, there is almost a sense of not wanting to admit failure: the organizations spend so much effort and time in vetting recruits (or going from volunteer to part-time to full-time) that it is difficult to let go.

 Think About It: How do you find toxins in your culture? And then, what do you do?

Chapter 16

Is The Culture Working?

What gets measured gets done.

Jim Giuffre
Chief operating officer,
Healthwise

As Jim Giuffre, COO of Healthwise put it, "If you match metrics with expectations, you can reinforce the culture." The key for creative for leaders is to measure progress so that it helps encourage behaviors and the environment they want. At Healthwise, they count "mission points," or how many times a day people use Healthwise information to make better health decisions. For Boise State basketball, Ryan Lundgren points to a full wall graphic that measures defensive moves—from rebounds to blocks—to show how the program is increasing focus on detail, execution and consistency. Finally, when he was Boise State's head football coach, Chris Petersen used a weekly written test of players to assess their knowledge and understanding of culture.

MIT professor Edgar Schein talked years ago about how to encourage people in organizations to change mindsets and behaviors. As he wrote, simply telling people that an organization needs to change, is in trouble, or faces an uncertain environment is not enough. Employees have to realize that if they do *not* learn something new and make a change, they and the organization will fail. They will be jobless or at least feel very anxious.

But even more important, leaders cannot ask people in their organizations to change if they are not willing to change themselves. They cannot force others to learn something new without doing so as well. And this means knowing where the organization and its members stand. That's why having observable behaviors is so critical. Several organizations have found some ways to track changes in culture even if they are not quantitative.

The Law Enforcement Agency of Choice

Early in the process of building an anti-complacency culture at the Ada County jail, Sheriff Gary Raney mentioned the phrase "We are the law enforcement agency of choice." When it began to stick in and outside of the organization, it became a way to define the behaviors that individuals were expected to show in their interactions with stakeholders on the outside, whether people who had been arrested or the citizen on the street. That included the people working at the front desk of the headquarters building.

The sheriff's office lobby is not a cozy place but it is professional. The floor is concrete and in the waiting area are several wooden benches that look like they were once pews in a church. To one side is an information board, with current and historical information. A glass fronted desk sits at the back of the room, where visitors check in. It's intimidating, though. The glass is thick, there's a mouse hole opening to talk through, and you must lean in to speak. Despite all of this, the office wanted to convey the idea of being "the law enforcement agency of choice" with a culture of service to others. Employees were expected to be as welcoming and helpful as they could to anyone who showed up, whether they were visiting one of the senior staff, an inmate, or asking about where to get a concealed weapons permit.

Raney noticed one employee did not fit the mold of being welcoming. Over a couple of weeks, he watched her behavior and found nearly a dozen actions that were unacceptable, from waiting for others on the front desk to answer the phone instead of doing it herself, to not looking up when a patron approached the window, to making the person wait for what seemed like a long time before acknowledgement. Then, even as she was talking, she did not look the person in the eye. All were observable behaviors that conveyed the message: You are not important. And they certainly did not convey to the public that this was an "agency of choice."

Once he'd tracked the behaviors, Raney met with the employee and told her what he'd seen and tracked. He made it clear that these were behaviors that must change within the next two weeks or she would be looking for another job.

Raney and other leaders know that they cannot always influence the thinking of employees, but if they can measure observable behaviors, they can urge changes in that. He focuses on how to measure actions and events that enhance, or hurt the culture and then uses data-based evidence to make improvements. Not anecdotes not "hunches," not opinions, but data.

Cortney Dennis, the head of dispatch, noted that Raney applies that thinking all across the sheriff's office units. In her area, a key measure is 911-answer time. The national average for answering a 911 call is 90% within 10 seconds. Raney challenged Dennis and her team to set a higher goal, which they did: answering 92% of all 911 calls within 10 seconds. Then, she said, they measure it:

> *Quarterly, we can look at our percentages to see why they have gone up and why they may be lower. The sheriff is*

always looking for ways to improve our performance, to really BE the law enforcement agency of choice that people look to.

Clear to understand, clear to measure, and makes a subtle argument about the importance of being service focused, with a culture that supports being "the law enforcement agency of choice."

Iron Sharpens Iron

Boise State head football coach Bryan Harsin wants his players to be competitive, to be scrappy and to want to win, badly. He also wants them to get excited about winning and scoring when it happens. He points to the change he saw over six weeks in his first spring as he tried to instill a sense of winning and excitement during spring football season. As he puts it, "Iron sharpens iron," and he wants the players to be tough on themselves and tough on each other but still relish winning. That will help players improve.

In the first three weeks of spring ball, he noticed trigger points that convinced him the players were beginning to "get it." At the first scrimmage, when someone scored, the players showed no reaction, no celebration. Harsin said that *everyone* should celebrate and get excited when a score happened. During the second scrimmage, he thought that players "faked" celebration: they cheered at scores but "were not really into it." Harsin jumped on them again, saying they needed to get excited in a real way. By the third scrimmage, he says, the players—all of them—were excited, yelling, and celebrating when any score happened. Three weeks later, at the end of spring ball, the students were kidding with each other, getting scrappy, and Harsin felt some of competitiveness was back. He wants them to be pushing each other to get better, being demanding enough to get tougher, but also celebrating and really getting a sense of wanting to win built into their play and their attitudes. His measure, then, of how well the culture of "iron sharpening iron" is emerging. Given that his first season at Boise State led to a winning bowl game, he's on the way to building the culture he wants.

Interestingly, though, Harsin is realistic about a full change in mindset. The initial spurt of scrimmage enthusiasm needed time to translate into ongoing long-lasting change in the way players think and act. He has drawn on student leaders to help make that happen but even so, he expects it could take up to two years.

On the Field or on the Bench?

At WhiteCloud Analytics, part of the developer subculture is a bit competitive, across developers and among the teams. It pushes people to work hard and beat the competition. The internal competition emerges often in terms of being accountable to each other: "You say you'll complete a section of code and you'd better do it or you'll let the team down."

To measure and then show that publically (at least within the firm), one development team created a "football field" to illustrate whether they had achieved what they'd promised in any given week. In the company conference room, the team has posted a photo of the iconic blue Boise State football field. On magnets are photos of the team's faces—smiling and frowning. If a person achieves his or her promised goals for the week, she may put her smiling face "onto the field." If she's not accomplished what was promised, the frowning face "sits on the bench" at the bottom of the photo.

Peer pressure and public measurement. It fits the culture of working for that team, but also brings a bit of toughness and being pushed. Other organizational leaders would blanche at the thought of making anyone "sit on the bench" in a public way, but for this firm and this culture, measuring and showing the results to everyone works.

WhiteCloud's leadership team values creativity, innovation and the ability to be strategic thinkers. That translates into looking ahead, watching for and anticipating trends that could affect the industry and company. Director of administration, Natalie Shores, sees a connection between the value of looking ahead and how people show up to meetings. How many times does it take, she asks herself and others in the leadership team, when someone says "we didn't think of that" before a group starts to question whether they have fully embraced the value of strategic thinking? How many times does it take for the leadership team to talk about the link between tasks and the long term goal before organizational members begin to talk about the connections without being prompted?

Similarly, Metageek, a Boise, Idaho, tech firm wants to instill an innovative but "accomplishment focused" culture. Metageek's culture values openness. Instead of holding meetings where engineers talk about progress, CEO Ryan Woodings and his leadership team decided to devote an entire white board wall to the effort. So for a time, the firm used a white board wall with three columns to show project progress: to do, in progress, and done. The board was covered with pink and blue and green and yellow Post-it notes, all indicating what stage the projects were in. Transparency, urgency, and getting it done came through on the seven foot tall chart, emphasizing several pieces of the firm's culture at the same time.

The Full Experience

Bishop Kelly President Rich Raimondi came from a background in business and was convinced that schools, like companies, have customers who want good experiences. His school colleagues, however, resisted comparing a company to a school and were reluctant to think about students and parents and donors as "customers." He waited, hired a new key leader, and developed a stronger culture that matched what he wanted for the school.

Finally, after about four years, he raised the topic again, this time after discussion about retention and why some students and families were leaving the school. At that point, trust and transparency levels were high and his colleagues and others were ready to think about customer experience.

So one day Raimondi asked them to think about the full experience of a family with a child in the school, from the time they went to the website to learn about the school, to the first phone call, to the interview with the enrollment manager and teachers and administrators to the first days of the student. Then, he asked them to imagine what the student's experience would be like, in and out of the classroom, whether the environment felt caring and supportive, how the student built (or did not) a connection with the community. As he talked through the notion of examining the full experience, he also emphasized that every person in the school community played a role, from the custodians, teachers and staff, to the students, parents and donors. At that point, he says, the importance of, responsibility for, and accountability to the culture became clear. Not quantifiable, but measurable in terms of the ways people behaved.

The Value of Touch

Boise State basketball coach Leon Rice claims that physical touch can make a difference in how players play but perhaps also in reflecting the culture. The coaches film all practices and then review them with players. Rice has read that professional teams have found that the more "touches" (physically) players have with each other, the better the teams play. That includes anything from a pat on the back to high-fives to huddles. It shows engagement, support, and involvement.

So he talked to his players about "touches" and then showed them their practice films. In one practice, two players contrasted dramatically. One seemed engaged, excited, and did well in practice. The other seemed uninvolved, distracted and did not play well. It showed on the film.

During that practice, the engaged player had touched other players twenty-three times; the unengaged player had two touches. As Rice said, "he was on an island" that day, very unengaged and not playing well. Such a visual example of how to "feel" and measure the culture was easy for his players to grasp.

What Have You Done for me Lately?

Finally, two software firms use an approach that links an employee's performance evaluation to whether or not he or she is explicitly contributing to the values and culture of the firm. Metageek leaders assess each employee on how he or she contributes to the values of the firm. Three key values are "make it better," "do the dishes" (as in carry your own weight in the organization), or "progress over perfection." Employees receive ratings of "great, good, or getting better" on each value. The key is for them to realize that contribution to the broader good of the organization is critical, and thus their "fit" and behaviors that support those values and culture are fundamental to their success at the company.

Somewhat similar, WhiteCloud uses an approach called "net contribution," presented as an equation:

Job Contribution - Friction = Net Contribution

The firm's leaders assess employees on what they have contributed to the performance of the organization but also assess them on the "hassle factor," or how much friction an employee may create during the work process. The difference between contribution and friction then generates what the firm leaders refer to as "net contribution," and they've used the evaluation to increase (or not) salaries. Thus, if a person is a great performer but high-maintenance—a huge time sink or complainer, demanding a lot of hand-holding or coddling—the overall contribution is less. By explicitly taking into account, or in a sense "measuring," the actions of employees that support, or do not, values and culture, it conveys the message that companies take values and culture seriously enough to measure how employees support them.

In contrast, an employee who carries out her job as expected but then goes beyond expectations to help another unit in the firm, to do something unasked for that makes a contribution, or to make the organization a more positive place to work, has a low friction score. That employee could receive more in compensation to reflect that high level of net contribution.

Think About It: What are three ways that you "know" or measure what's happening in your culture? How do you tell if it is the one you want?

Summary of Grow The Culture

It does not matter how slowly you go, as long as you do not stop.

Confucius
Philosopher (551 B.C.- 479 B.C.)

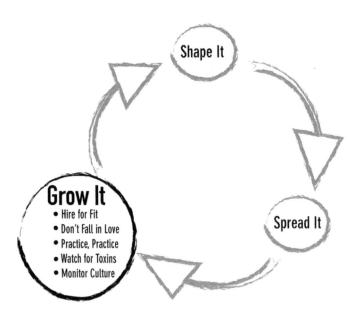

Shape It
- Lay Foundation
- Add Nutrients
- Insert Behaviors

The Competitive Advantage

Spread It
- Hear It
- See It
- Do It
- Teach It
- Feel It

Grow It
- Hire for Fit
- Don't Fall in Love
- Practice, Practice
- Watch for Toxins
- Monitor Culture

Sum It Up

In leaving something unsaid, the beholder is given a chance to complete the idea.

Okakura Kakuzo
Author
The Book of Tea (1956 edition)

We've said much in this book but also left much for you to make your own. We offer a few key points here as the basis for you to use as you "complete the idea" of growing culture in your own organization:

- Be deliberate in the process and throughout the process.
- Stay focused on culture or you'll lose it.
- Give the process time.
- Use culture as a competitive advantage.

We wish you good luck in your own petri dish.

Acknowledgements

In the course of this project, we tried to "grow the culture we wanted." We wanted to do things differently, to be open to new ideas, and to test out ones we thought worked (and often found they did not). That meant finding the right people who would put their hearts and minds into it and then, giving them leeway. In that process, research assistants Shanshan Bai, Kelsey Crow, and Jackie Presnell helped with interviews and analysis, and likely had no idea of the wild ride they were in for and yet they've come through in ways far beyond expectations. They contributed key "aha moments" in our discussions, maintained an upbeat approach even when the project seemed chaotic, and grew as young researchers along the way.

Stephanie Chism maintained a steady course for all of us during the process while Josh Davis, Joanna Lui, and Madison Motzner guided the production of the book from start to finish. Jesse Baker helped with interviews and translated sports lingo into regular language.

Many people acted as sounding boards, letting us test out ideas, changing and challenging them and we appreciate the help, especially from colleagues at Aalborg University in Denmark, Boise State University and beyond, including Rob Anson, Mark Bathrick, Linda Clark-Santos, Jim Giuffre, Steve Hatten, Bob Lokken, Steve Moorcroft, Jim Munger, Bill Napier, Tony Olbrich, Dan Salamone, Kirk Smith, Jeremiah Shinn, Rich Stuppy, Sully Taylor, and Angeli Weller. Nancy's strategic management MBA 546 students during fall 2014 also pushed and shaped and helped many ideas become clearer. Members of several of learning gangs we work with in Boise were also instrumental, including The Posse, The Huddle, The Sidewinders, The Wranglers, and especially The Hard Rock Miners who spent almost a year discussing culture (Gary Allen, Jessica Flynn, John McFarlane, Kate Pape, Dale Pike, Peter Vomocil). We spoke with several members of the former Trey McIntyre Project, including Brian Aune, Chanel DaSilva, Christina Johnson, Jane Naillon, and Rachel Sherak. An unexpected treat was working with the first cohort of Boise State University's Athletic Leadership program, in particular, Taylor Anguiano, Breann Crowell, Travis Haug, Jocelyn Perry, Catherine Tisler, and Katelin Wollner. Thanks to Tyler Johnson and Scott Moorcroft for organizing that opportunity.

Of course, the organizational leaders and members who were kind enough to give us their time and insights shine throughout the book. The reciprocal learning between people inside of organizations and those who study organizations is often some of the best part of working on a book project.

The College of Business and Economics, Boise State University and the community of Boise, Idaho, have long supported work with The Gang. While Gang members and their organizations have changed over the years, the common thread is that these are highly creative, high performing organizations full of aggressive learners who are relentlessly curious and who also are high output/low ego people. We hope that never changes as they all try to do things differently to get better.

References and Further Reading

Introduction

Page 5: Bryant, A. "The Culture Always Comes First," *The New York Times*, 21 December 2014: B2.

Page 13: Stone, B. and Satariano, A. "Tim Cook Interview: The iPhone 6, the Apple Watch, and Remaking a Company's Culture," *Bloomberg*. September 17, 2014, http://www.bloomberg.com/news/features/2014-09-17/tim-cook-interview-the-iphone-6-the-apple-watch-and-remaking-a-companys-culture-i077npsy

Part I: Shape The Culture

Page: 27: Bryant, A. "Jess Lee of Polyvore on the Value of Simplicity." *The New York Times*, November 21, 2013: B2.

Page 27: Bryant, A. "When Humility and Audacity Go Hand in Hand." *The New York Times*, September 30, 2012: B2.

Page 33: Goleman, D. 1995. *Emotional Intelligence*. New York City: Bantam Books.

Page 33: Fredrickson, B.L. and Losada, M. "Positive affect and the complex dynamics of human flourishing." *American Psychologist,* Volume 60: (2005) 678-686.

Page 35: Bryant, A. "A Good Manager Must Be More Than a Messenger." *The New York Times,* May 30, 2013: B2.

Part II: Spread The Culture

Page 47: --. "Backwards and Forwards," *The Economist,* 3 September 2011: 81.

Hear it

Page 52: Cilley, M.. " Petersen talks about post, future at Boise State," *Idaho Statesman,* July 31, 2013: S1.

See it

Page 58: Carr, N. *The Shallows.* New York City: W.W. Norton, 2010.

Page 59: Silverman R.E. "Doodling for Dollars: Firms Try to Get Gadget-Obsessed Workers to Look Up—and Sketch Ideas," *The Wall Street Journal,* April 25, 2012: B7.

Page 59: Hansegard, J. "IKEA's New Catalogs: Less Pine, More Pixels," *The Wall Street Journal,* August 23, 2012: B1.

Page 60: Chen, B.X. "Simplifying the Bull: How Picasso Helps to Teach Apple's Style," *The New York Times,* August 10, 2014: A1, B6.

Page 66: Kandel, E.R. "What the Brain Can Tell Us About Art," *The New York Times*, April 12, 2013, http://www.nytimes.com/2013/04/14/opinion/sunday/what-the-brain-can-tell-us-about-art.html?_r=0

Feel it

Page 78: Killeffer, L. "Design & Innovation with Robert Fabricant, Frog Design." *Innovation Excellence*, February 24, 2013: 7-8.

Page 78: Cron, L. *Wired for Story: The Writer's Guide to Using Brain Science to Hook Readers from the Very First Sentence.* Berkeley, CA: Ten Speed Press, 2012.

Page 79: Malone, M.S. "How to Avoid a Bonfire of the Humanities," *The Wall Street Journal*, October 24, 2012: A17.

Page 81: *The Heartmath Institute* (heartmath.org) reports on research and ways to use different types of energy in positive ways.

Page 82-83: Sebesta, C. 2012 "Three Local Companies put Creativity in their Spaces and their Work," *Austin American-Statesman*, June 28, 2014.

Page 83: Lublin, J. S. "Can a New Culture Fix Troubled Companies?," *The Wall Street Journal*, March 12, 2013: B1.

Page 83: --. "Beyond the Cubicle," *The Wall Street Journal*, August 3, 2012: C12.

Page 87: Cuddy, A. "Your body language shapes who you are." *TED Talks*. June 2012. Video.

Part III: Grow The Culture

Hiring for fit but Vet for Values

Page 97: Bryant, A. "Amy Errett of Madison Reed, on Finding Your Genius," *The New York Times,* November 15, 2013: B2.

Page 98: Bryant, A. "The First Rule of Brainstorming: Suspend Disbelief," *The New York Times,* January 19, 2013, BU2.

Don't Fall in Love

Page 101: Sitkin, S.B. and Hackman, J.R. 2011. "Developing Team Leadership: An Interview with Coach Mike Krzyzewski," *Academy of Management Learning and Education,* 10.3 (2011): 496.

Is The Culture Working?

Page 117: Schein, E.H. "How Can Organizations Learn Faster? The Challenge of Entering The Green Room," *Sloan Management Review,* Winter 1993: 85-92.

About the Authors

Nancy K. Napier, Distinguished professor and director of the Centre for Creativity and Innovation at Boise State University and adjunct professor at Aalborg University (Denmark), scours the world for ideas—from Vietnam to Botswana. Mostly, she loves the ones from The Gang and its offshoots and hopes this book will inspire wise gangs to spring up everywhere.

Jamie Cooper, CEO of Drake Cooper, has helped his firm achieve many professional awards, whistles on his bike as he rides to work, and, if he ever needed a new career, could do impressions.

Mark Hofflund, managing director of the Idaho Shakespeare Festival and a board member for the National Endowment of the Arts, ran track for Princeton in college, and manages stage wildlife with aplomb, as in deer, geese, and skunks.

Don Kemper, founder and CEO of Healthwise, is a regular national and international speaker on consumer healthcare issues, invites well-behaved dogs to join their owners at work, and walks more miles than most people drive.

Bob Lokken, founder and CEO of WhiteCloud Analytics, has given in to being an unrelenting serial entrepreneur who once tried to retire to play golf but decided that was harder work than starting new firms.

Rich Raimondi, president of Bishop Kelly High School, retired after decades as an executive at Hewlett-Packard.

But rather than retirement, he decided "returnment" was more his style and so jumped into education and has never looked back.

Gary Raney, sheriff of the Ada County Sheriff's Office, once said an inmate's escape was a *good* thing—to help the office throw off complacency. His untapped talent is organizing competitive cooking events.

Leon Rice, head basketball coach at Boise State University, pushes his players to excel but when he needs to, he can swish a shot from center court, just to show he can.

John Michael Schert, visiting artist and social entrepreneur, teaches creative process to MBA students at the University of Chicago's Booth School of Business, and must be the only international dancer who also played a mean game of high school football in Valdosta, Georgia.

23037025R00085

Made in the USA
Middletown, DE
14 August 2015